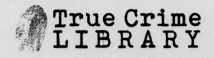
True Crime LIBRARY

Mass MURDERERS

DRUG CARTELS AND SMUGGLERS
INFAMOUS TERRORISTS
MASS MURDERERS
MODERN-DAY PIRATES
ORGANIZED CRIME
SERIAL KILLERS

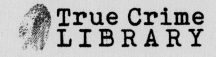

True Crime LIBRARY

Mass MURDERERS

RUDOLPH T. HEIts

ELDORADO INK

Eldorado Ink
PO Box 100097
Pittsburgh, PA 15233
www.eldoradoink.com

Produced by OTTN Publishing, Stockton, New Jersey

CPSIA compliance information: Batch#CS2013-3. For further information, contact Eldorado Ink at info@eldoradoink.com.

First printing

1 3 5 7 9 8 6 4 2

Library of Congress Cataloging-in-Publication Data
available from the Library of Congress

ISBN-13: 978-1-61900-034-6 (hc)
ISBN-13: 978-1-61900-035-3 (trade)
ISBN-13: 978-1-61900-036-0 (ebook)

For information about custom editions, special sales, or premiums, please contact our special sales department at info@eldoradoink.com.

TABLE OF CONTENTS

MaSS MURDERERS
An InTRODUCTION

Though she'd been in the United States Congress for less than a year, Gabrielle Giffords was hardly a political novice when she hosted a meet-and-greet event for constituents on August 25, 2007. Before winning election to Arizona's Eighth Congressional District, Giffords had served as a state representative and state senator. Genial and vivacious, she connected easily with all types of people. Yet Giffords could hardly have known how to respond to one questioner at her August 25 event. "What is government," the young man asked, "if words have no meaning?"

Giffords did her best to answer, and her office later sent a letter thanking the questioner for his attendance at the event. But the young man, Jared Lee Loughner, wasn't satisfied. He complained to friends about the congresswoman's supposed refusal to answer his question. He branded Giffords a fake.

Friends and acquaintances had already begun to notice personality changes in Loughner, who was a couple weeks shy of his 19th birthday at the time of his interaction with Representative Giffords. In the years that followed, he would spiral into full-blown mental illness. He was eventually diagnosed with paranoid schizophrenia.

Loughner blamed the government for all sorts of wrongdoing—including, as he said on a video he posted to YouTube, effecting "mind control and brainwash on the people by controlling grammar." For some reason, however, he reserved special enmity for Gabby Giffords.

On the morning of January 8, 2011, a few days after being sworn in for her third term in the U.S. House of Representatives, Giffords held a "Congress on Your Corner" event in the

7

On January 8, 2011, Jared Lee Loughner (below) killed six people and injured 13 others during his attack at a political event in Tuscon, Arizona. Among his victims were U.S. Congresswoman Gabrielle Giffords (left), who survived with severe injuries, and nine-year-old Christina-Taylor Green (inset). In November 2012, Loughner (below) pled guilty and was sentenced to life in prison without the possibility of parole.

parking lot of a supermarket near Tucson. At 10:10, a little over an hour after the event had begun, Jared Lee Loughner strode toward the table Giffords had set up. He pulled out a Glock 9mm semiautomatic pistol and, from a few feet away, shot Giffords in the head. Then he began firing into the small crowd that had turned out to meet the congresswoman. Bystanders managed to subdue the gunman only after he'd emptied a 33-round clip and was attempting to reload.

Miraculously, Gabby Giffords would survive her head wound. Of the 18 others hit by gunfire, however, 6 were killed. Twenty-two-year-old Jared Lee Loughner had joined the ranks of America's mass murderers.

To be classified as a mass murderer, according to the Federal Bureau of Investigation, an offender must kill at least four people in a single incident at the same location. This simple definition could encompass a wide range of killers—from an armed robber who murders to eliminate witnesses, to a gang member involved in a shoot-out with a rival group, to a terrorist who blows up a building, to a person who guns down random strangers after suffering some personal setback. It's examples like the last one, however, that most laypeople have in mind when they talk about mass murder. Many criminologists, too, focus on similar types of cases, and some specifically exclude from the category of mass murder homicides committed in the course of a separate crime, homicides committed in furtherance of a criminal enterprise, or terrorism-related homicides.

One category of multiple-victim murderer closely related to the mass murderer is the spree killer. The primary difference between the two involves where the murders are committed. A spree killer is defined as an offender who murders at least four people over a relatively short period of time, but at more than one location. William Cruse is an example. Cruse, a retired librarian in Palm Bay, Florida, believed people were spreading rumors he was gay. On April 23, 1987, Cruse grabbed his rifle, shotgun, and pistol and hopped into his car. He stopped to shoot a neighborhood boy who was outside playing basketball, then headed for a nearby supermarket. There Cruse killed three people and wounded several others before driving to another supermarket. He wounded many people and killed three, including two police officers, before barricading himself inside the store with a hostage. Police eventually dislodged the 59-year-old with tear gas.

Some criminologists don't believe it's particularly useful to distinguish between mass murderers and spree killers. For one thing, the geographic parameters are subject to interpretation. How far does a killer have to travel before a single location becomes multiple locations? Would a gunman who shot people on one street, then walked around the block to shoot more people still be considered at the same location? More fundamentally, if a perpetrator commits a group of killings as part of the same unfolding event, does it matter whether some victims are cut down in one place and other victims die some distance away? Following that logic, this book includes several cases that might technically be classified as spree killings. For instance, Charles Whitman killed his wife and mother in their respective homes the night before he shot dozens of people at the University of Texas. In 2012, Adam Lanza killed his mother at home before driving to Sandy Hook Elementary School, where he murdered 26 children and six adults.

Experts say that there is no single psychological profile of a mass murderer. In terms of their mental states and their motivations, mass murderers vary widely. Many show signs of mental illness (though a definitive diagnosis is often impossible because the murderer has been killed). Some mass murderers suffer from psychosis, a distorted perception of reality which may include paranoia, delusions, or hallucinations and which is characteristic of severe mental illness such as schizophrenia. A small number may be clinical psychopaths—essentially, people without a conscience. Many, if not most, mass murderers suffer from chronic depression. Not surprisingly, many think about ending their own lives. "I never came across one [mass murderer] who wasn't at least partially interested in suicide," observed forensic psychiatrist and criminologist Park Dietz.

But depression in people who become mass murderers is typically paired with deep-seated anger. And that anger gets focused outward. Mass murderers almost always have a profound sense of aggrievement. They blame their problems, setbacks, and disappointments on other people. They see themselves as victims. A murderous rampage, then, can fulfill two functions for the angry depressive: ending his own misery (most mass murderers plan to die at the scene of their killings, either by suicide or at the hands of police), and exacting vengeance. "Before they die," notes criminologist Alan J. Fox, coauthor of *Extreme Killing: Understanding Serial and Mass Murder*, "it's very important for them to get some satisfaction, to get even with the people or the institutions or the world that has treated them so badly or made their life so miserable."

Thus Robert Stewart, unemployed and angry that his wife has left him, goes to the Carthage, North Carolina, nursing home where she works and murders a nurse and eight patients between the ages of 75 and 98. Stewart's wife survives the 2009 incident by hiding in a bathroom.

Thus part-time letter carrier Patrick Sherrill, repeatedly taken to task for misdirecting mail, responds to a reprimand from supervisors by slaughtering 14 coworkers the following day. The massacre takes place in 1986 in the small town of Edmond, Oklahoma.

Thus James Huberty, having suffered a string of financial setbacks and recently laid off from a menial job, declares to his wife, "Society had its chance." Huberty goes to a McDonald's restaurant near his home in the San Diego neighborhood of San Ysidro. There he kills 21 and wounds 19. The 1984 massacre still ranks as one of the bloodiest mass shootings in U.S. history.

Many people assume that mass murders such as these are spontaneous events that happen after the perpetrator "snaps." But that is erroneous. Mass murders almost always involve a degree of planning, and some killers plot their massacres meticulously for months. "Instead of snapping," says Michael Welner, associate professor of psychiatry at New York University School of Medicine, "imagine a cage that someone has the capacity to unhinge. They simply decide that today is the day."

An overwhelming majority of mass murderers—96.5 percent, according to recent estimates—are male. Several factors explain this. First of all, men are more violent generally. Men also tend to resort to violence when their status or self-esteem is challenged, while women are more likely to reserve violence for defensive situations. Women, moreover, tend to blame themselves for their problems. Whereas a depressed, humiliated, and angry man may plan a murder-suicide, a woman in the same situation is more likely just to commit suicide.

Mass murder can be, and is, committed with a variety of weapons. One killer profiled in this book, Richard Speck, used a knife; another, Andrew Kehoe, explosives. But firearms, particularly semiautomatic handguns, are the weapons of choice for the vast majority of mass murderers.

Almost every country has mass murders. Particularly shocking incidents from outside the United States include:

Flowers, flags, and candles were left outside the Oslo cathedral as a memorial to the victims of Anders Breivik's murderous rampage in July 2011.

- a 1996 attack on a kindergarten class in Dunblane, Scotland, by a disgruntled youth-club director named Thomas Hamilton. Hamilton killed 16 children and their teacher, and he wounded 15 other children.
- the 1996 massacre in Port Arthur, Tasmania, Australia, perpetrated by Martin Bryant, a young man with intellectual disabilities and a history of mental problems. Bryant killed 35 and wounded 21.
- the bombing of a government building and shooting massacre at a youth camp in Norway, carried out by Anders Breivik in 2011. Breivik, diagnosed with paranoid schizophrenia, claimed an astounding number of victims: 77 killed, 242 wounded.

Outside the United States, such incidents are regarded as anomalies. Australia, for example, hasn't had a single mass murder since the Port Arthur massacre. The United States averages about 20 incidents per year.

Some people suspect that cultural factors such as the ubiquity of violent movies and video games contribute to the higher incidence of mass murder in the United States. To date, however, research has yet to prove such a link.

A far more significant factor may be the easy availability of guns. By virtue of the Second Amendment to the Constitution, Americans have a right to possess firearms. For every 100 residents of the United States, there are about 89 civilian-owned guns. In no other country is gun ownership nearly that high. Furthermore, the types of weapons available to Americans are especially lethal. These include semiautomatic handguns and military-style rifles that are capable of firing five rounds a second and that can accommodate large-capacity magazines. Two especially horrifying incidents from 2012 reminded Americans of the carnage such weapons can produce.

On the night of Thursday, July 19, moviegoers in Aurora, Colorado, flocked to the Century 16 multiplex. The attraction was a midnight premiere of *The Dark Knight Rises*, the latest offering in the popular Batman franchise.

James Holmes, who took a seat in the front row of theater 9, had purchased his ticket nearly two weeks earlier. The 24-year-old, who had recently dropped out of a Ph.D. neuroscience program after failing an important exam, sported hair dyed a flaming red hue. But he didn't especially stand out—other people in the packed theater were wearing Batman-themed costumes.

About 20 minutes into the movie,

The .223 caliber AR-15 rifle, which was used in the December 2012 mass murder at Sandy Hook Elementary, is one of the most popular semiautomatic rifles available for sale in the United States. According to the Bureau of Alcohol, Tobacco and Firearms (ATF), more than 2 million AR-15 rifles were sold between 2000 and 2010.

The Aurora, Colorado, theater where James Holmes killed a dozen people in July 2012. The mug shot above, taken the night Holmes was arrested, shows the killer with red-dyed hair; this may have been done so he would resemble the Joker, a villain from the Batman comics and films.

Holmes left the theater via an emergency exit. He made sure to prop the door open so he could get back inside. When he returned, at approximately 12:37 AM, he was dressed all in black, with body armor and a gas mask. He carried a fearsome arsenal: a Smith and Wesson M&P15 semiautomatic rifle, with a 100-round drum magazine; a Remington pump-action 12-gauge shotgun; and at least one Glock .40-caliber semiautomatic pistol. Holmes tossed a tear-gas grenade into the theater, then began blasting away with his shotgun.

In the darkened theater, many audience members initially thought they were witnessing some sort of hoax or publicity stunt for *The Dark Knight*. But as the awful reality became apparent, frantic people dove to the floor or raced toward the exits. Holmes calmly fired his semiautomatic rifle. Many bullets from the high-powered weapon tore through multiple victims; other rounds went through the walls and wounded people in the adjacent theater. After he'd fired 30 rounds from his rifle, the drum magazine jammed. Holmes switched to his Glock.

Police were on the scene by 12:40 and had the building surrounded two minutes later. Around 12:46 officers apprehended Holmes just outside the back of the theater. He appeared calm and offered no resistance.

The rampage, which lasted perhaps eight minutes, claimed 12 lives. Fifty-eight people were wounded. Investigators would later determine that Holmes had planned the massacre for at least two months. No motive was immediately apparent, though speculation centered on the shooter's frustration with his academic failures.

It's possible that no motive will ever be known for the massacre perpetrated by 20-year-old Adam Lanza in Newtown, Connecticut, on December 14, 2012. That morning Lanza shot his mother, Nancy, four times in the head

A memorial for the 26 children and adults killed by Adam Lanza during the massacre at Sandy Hook Elementary School in Connecticut on December 14, 2012.

as she lay in her bed. He collected four weapons belonging to his mother and drove to nearby Sandy Hook Elementary School. He left one weapon, a shotgun, in the car and approached the school entrance carrying a Bushmaster semiautomatic AR-15 rifle. In his pockets he had plenty of extra 30-round magazines for the rifle as well as two semiautomatic pistols, a 9mm Glock and a 10mm Sig Sauer.

As part of a recently enacted set of security measures, the school's doors were locked when Lanza arrived around 9:35 AM. He got into the building by shooting out a window. Hearing the noise, Sandy Hook's principal, Dawn Hochsprung, and school psychologist Mary Sherlach went to investigate. They tried to stop Lanza but were both gunned down.

In a first-grade classroom, Lanza slaughtered substitute teacher Lauren Rousseau and 15 of her 16 students. The lone survivor played dead. In another first-grade classroom Lanza killed teacher Victoria Leigh Soto as she tried to shield students who were running away. He also killed six of Soto's students.

Behavioral therapist Rachel D'Avino, who had just started working at Sandy Hook, was killed as she tried to shield a student. So, too, was teacher's aide Ann Marie Murphy.

Around 9:49 AM, after seeing police officers approach, Lanza killed himself with a gunshot to the head. He'd snuffed out the lives of 20 six- and seven-year-olds, along with six adults.

Adam Lanza

In January 2013, in the aftermath of the Sandy Hook massacre, President Obama announced a series of executive actions and proposed legislation to curb gun violence in the United States. The legislative proposals included a requirement that all firearms purchasers undergo a criminal background check; a ban on military-style "assault weapons"; and a 10-round limit on ammunition magazines. Even if Congress enacted the legislation—which was by no means assured—nobody expected it to be a panacea. But perhaps, supporters hoped, the measures might reduce mass murder's awful toll.

ANDREW KEHOE
THE Bath SCHOOL Disaster

Americans have a long and venerable tradition of complaining about their taxes. But perhaps no one has ever taken resentment of a high tax bill to greater extremes than Andrew Kehoe. Incensed that his property taxes had been increased to pay for a new school, and thwarted in his repeated efforts to get those taxes lowered, Kehoe packed the school with explosives and blew it up. Eighty-five years later, the atrocity remains the deadliest school-related massacre in U.S. history.

Andrew Kehoe was 47 years old in 1919, the year he and his wife, Nellie, moved onto a farm outside the rural town of Bath, Michigan. Kehoe didn't especially like farming—he'd been trained as an electrician and enjoyed nothing more than tinkering with machines. But the farm became available on the death of his wife's uncle, and

Kehoe put down $6,000 in cash and took out a $6,000 mortgage to purchase the land.

Bath, located about 10 miles northeast of the state capital of Lansing, was a small community. It had fewer than 300 residents, and a one-room schoolhouse accommodated all the school-age children from the town and the surrounding farms.

One-room schoolhouses had long been the norm in rural America. But during the first decades of the 20th century, education reformers began advocating for the creation of larger, consolidated schools, which would make possible the instruction of students by grade level. This, the reformers argued, was inherently more effective than teaching children from kindergarten to high school in the same classroom.

Many communities, however, resisted school consolidation. In Bath

Township, population about 7,500, the issue was contentious. For his part, Andrew Kehoe stood among the most vehement opponents of consolidation. He and his wife were childless, and Kehoe saw no need for a big new school to replace the one-room schoolhouses dotting the 35-square-mile township. But in 1922, after several years of public discussion and debate, supporters of consolidation prevailed. Bath Township voters approved the formation of a consolidated school district, and a bond was issued to fund construction of a new school.

Bath Consolidated School, located near the town of Bath, opened in November 1922. It had a total enrollment of 236.

Bath Township residents saw their property taxes jump by 50 percent in 1923, as the township began paying off its school bond. Andrew Kehoe wasn't about to accept that state of affairs lying down. He assailed township officials over the assessed value of his farm, which he claimed was too high. He also campaigned for and was elected to the school board in 1924. Throughout his three-year term, he served as treasurer of the board. He continually harangued the board about the need to lower school taxes.

Other members of the school board considered Kehoe competent, but exceedingly difficult to work with and at

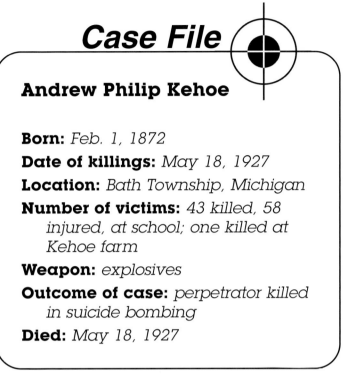

Case File

Andrew Philip Kehoe

Born: *Feb. 1, 1872*
Date of killings: *May 18, 1927*
Location: *Bath Township, Michigan*
Number of victims: *43 killed, 58 injured, at school; one killed at Kehoe farm*
Weapon: *explosives*
Outcome of case: *perpetrator killed in suicide bombing*
Died: *May 18, 1927*

times petulant. He became enraged if he didn't get his way. He questioned every expenditure, no matter how routine. And, for reasons that aren't entirely clear, he pursued a vendetta against the school superintendent, Emory Huyck. Even after the rest of the school board had rebuffed his attempt to oust Huyck, Kehoe continued to subject the superintendent to constant (though apparently baseless) accusations of financial impropriety. He also snubbed Huyck at every opportunity.

In 1925 Bath's township clerk died shortly after taking office. The township board appointed Kehoe to serve in the post pending elections the following spring. As 1926 approached, Kehoe decided to run for a regular term as township clerk. He lost the election. Kehoe, according to his neighbor Monty Ellsworth, was furious at the public rejection.

Meanwhile, pressures mounted in Kehoe's private life. His wife, who suffered from tuberculosis, was in and out of the hospital. The farm failed to prosper—largely, neighbors would say, because Kehoe shunned hard work and accepted methods in favor of exotic techniques of his own devising. For example, he rigged two mowers behind his tractor in an attempt to reduce his cutting time by half. But the setup proved unwieldy, and large swaths of hay were left uncut. Instead of going back to finish the job, Kehoe simply left the hay standing. As he found it more difficult to pay his bills, Kehoe approached his bank with the bizarre request that the balance on his mortgage be forgiven because he'd paid too much for the farm. Needless to say, the request was denied. Kehoe also hectored Bath Township officials to lower his property taxes, but they continued to refuse.

For a while, Kehoe had served as an unofficial caretaker for Bath Consolidated School. He did odd jobs like fixing plumbing and getting rid of a swarm of bees. During the summer of 1926, Kehoe was hired to wire the school for electricity. To facilitate this

work, he was given a key to the building. He had access to all areas of the building at all hours.

Kehoe began loading into the basement large quantities of dynamite and pyrotol, an explosive that produces a fiery blast when combined with TNT. His repeated purchases of explosives and blasting caps didn't arouse suspicion because many farmers of the time blasted out tree trunks or large rocks on their land. By the spring of 1927 Kehoe had created two 500-pound bombs, one under the north wing and one under the south wing of the school.

Kehoe stopped paying his mortgage, and his bank began foreclosure proceedings. Investigators would later conclude that if Kehoe had simply sold his farm equipment, he could have paid off his mortgage entirely. But he wasn't thinking about the long term.

On the morning of May 18, 1927, Kehoe went to Bath Consolidated School. "He was working on a door, and he smiled at us as we walked in," Willis Cressman, then a high school student, would recall many years later.

After classes began, at 8:30, Kehoe drove back to his farm, which was about a half mile away. Sometime earlier, he'd smashed in his wife's skull with a blunt object. He'd placed her body in a wheelbarrow inside the chicken coop. Kehoe's horses were inside the barn, their legs bound together so that it would be

Concerned neighbors sort through the ruins of the Bath Consolidated School, destroyed by a powerful bomb on May 18, 1927.

impossible to rescue them. Kehoe had rigged the barn, along with the other buildings on his farm, with incendiary bombs. He set the bombs off, and in rapid succession the house, barn, and other buildings were engulfed in flames.

Seeing the fires, neighbors and a railroad crew working nearby rushed to Kehoe's farm to offer help. They found Kehoe remarkably unconcerned. He got

into his truck and, before driving away, told them they had better get to the school.

About 8:45, around the time Kehoe was leaving his farm, a massive explosion rocked Bath Consolidated. "After the first shock I thought for a moment I was blind," first-grade teacher Bernice Sterling later told a reporter. "When it came the air seemed to be full of children

The remains of Andrew Kehoe's car, destroyed in the explosion that took the bomber's life.

and flying desks and books. Children were tossed high in the air; some were catapulted out of the building."

Kehoe had set alarm clocks to detonate his bombs. Fortunately, a short circuit prevented one of the bombs from exploding, but the devastation was extensive nonetheless. The north wing of the school collapsed. Monty Ellsworth, who had a son in the second grade, jumped in his pickup and rushed to the school. What he found was appalling. "There was a pile of children of about five or six under the roof," Ellsworth recalled, "and some of them had arms sticking out, some had legs, and some just their heads sticking out. They were unrecognizable because they were covered with dust, plaster, and blood."

Ellsworth joined other local men who were trying to clear debris and rescue the trapped children and teachers. One of the men suggested that they drag the roof off the pile of rubble, and Ellsworth volunteered to drive to his farm to get some rope. On the road, he passed Kehoe, who flashed a wide grin as he drove past in his truck.

Several witnesses would report seeing Kehoe driving in or around town after the explosion. Ellsworth would later speculate that his neighbor was looking for people he wanted to kill, including another member of the school board and the bus driver, with whom he'd had several recent run-ins. Kehoe had a rifle in his truck.

About a half hour after the explosion, Kehoe pulled up in front of the school, where bedlam reigned. Students wandered about in a daze or lay on the ground bleeding. Frantic parents searched for their children. Rescue workers clawed through the rubble in a desperate effort to pull out survivors. Kehoe spotted Emory Huyck, and he and the school superintendent grappled briefly. Kehoe had packed his truck with explosives and small pieces of metal, and he detonated this bomb by firing his rifle into the truck. The blast killed Kehoe, Huyck, and several other people nearby.

Fire companies, doctors, nurses, and ambulances soon began arriving from Lansing. Several contractors sent all of their employees to Bath to help clear the debris and rescue those who were trapped. They worked all day, as did the medical professionals.

Despite these heroic efforts, the death toll was horrendous. Thirty-eight children, one teacher, and four other adults were killed in the two blasts at the school. Fifty-eight were injured. In the small community of Bath, no family was untouched by the tragedy.

Not surprisingly, many survivors would revile Kehoe for the rest of their lives. Some refused even to utter his name, which according to one woman "was like speaking an obscenity." Monty Ellsworth characterized his neighbor as "the world's worst demon."

For his part, Kehoe appeared to believe responsibility for his murderous actions rested elsewhere. At his destroyed farm, hanging on a wire fence, investigators found a neatly stenciled, handmade sign. "CRIMINALS ARE MADE, NOT BORN," it read.

HOWARD UNRUH
WALK OF DEATH

In the Cramer Hill neighborhood of Camden, New Jersey, Howard Unruh was considered eccentric. The 28-year-old had no friends. He had no job. He kept to himself, spending much of his time in the small second-floor apartment he shared with his mother, Freda. Neighborhood teens would sometimes taunt Unruh, calling him a "mama's boy." But mostly people left him alone and took little notice of what he did.

Unruh, by contrast, paid close attention to what fellow residents and shopkeepers on the 3200 block of River Road did, as well as what they said. Few of these people had any inkling that Unruh took umbrage at what they regarded as routine social interactions or a bit of small talk. But he seethed with resentment. He was convinced that, behind his back, neighbors were constantly disparaging him as a homo-

sexual. "They have been making derogatory remarks about my character," Unruh would claim.

Maurice and Rose Cohen were among the few neighbors with whom Unruh had an open dispute. The Cohens owned the River Road Pharmacy, living above the drugstore in quarters adjacent to Freda Unruh's apartment. Unruh would cut through their property to get to 32nd Street. They asked him to please close the gate when he did so. Unruh was offended. He complained about their 12-year-old son's trumpet practicing. The Cohens countered that Unruh played his radio too loudly.

In a diary, Unruh recorded the ways he believed the Cohens had wronged him. He also detailed the perceived slights he'd suffered at the hands of other neighbors. Next to some of the names in his diary, Unruh scribbled the abbreviation "retal." It stood for "retaliate."

According to his younger brother, James, Unruh hadn't always been so angry and isolated. "Since he came home from the service, he didn't seem to be the same," James Unruh declared. "He was nervous and never acted like his old self." During World War II, Howard Unruh had served in the U.S. Army as a tank gunner, seeing combat in North Africa, Italy, France, and Belgium.

Unruh had difficulty adjusting to civilian life after his honorable discharge from the army. He had several jobs, but never stayed very long at any of them. In 1948 he enrolled at Temple University in Philadelphia, intending to get a degree in pharmacy. However, he dropped out during his first semester. He never formulated another career plan or got another job. Instead he relied on his mother to support him. Their relationship was deeply troubled. According to psychiatrists who examined him later, Unruh harbored profound feelings of hostility toward his mother yet was physically attracted to her. He decided he must be gay, but he was intensely ashamed of that and didn't want anyone to know.

As early as 1947, Unruh had vague ideas about striking out against his perceived antagonists in Cramer Hill. Those ideas became increasingly focused during the summer of 1949, when family

Case File

Howard Barton Unruh

Born: *Jan. 21, 1921*
Date of killings: *Sept. 6, 1949*
Location: *Camden, N.J.*
Number of victims: *13 killed; 3 wounded*
Weapon: *Luger 9mm semiautomatic pistol*
Outcome of case: *committed to mental hospital*
Died: *Oct. 19, 2009*

members and acquaintances at the church he and his mother attended noted a marked decline in Unruh's mental state. He became increasingly paranoid. He muttered about plots by his neighbors to destroy him.

On Labor Day, Unruh went to a movie theater. He stayed there for many hours, sitting through a double feature three times. According to his later testimony, he believed one of the actresses was a neighbor he particularly despised. When he finally returned home early the following morning, he discovered that someone had stolen the gate he'd recently installed on the fence enclosing the small backyard of his mother's apartment. At that point, Unruh would

According to those who served with Unruh during the Second World War, he was a brave tank soldier. After he was honorably discharged from the U.S. Army in 1945, he returned home with his medals, including awards for marksmanship and sharpshooting. Unruh decorated his bedroom with military items, collected knives and firearms, and set up a place to practice pistol shooting in the basement of his mother's apartment.

confess, he decided to exact vengeance against his enemies that very day. He made a list of all the people he was going to kill.

Unruh had left the army as both an expert marksman and a gun enthusiast. In fact, one of his few pastimes was target practice in the basement of his building, where he'd set up a makeshift shooting range. Among his favorite weapons was a German Luger. He had accumulated more than 700 rounds of ammunition for the 9mm semiautomatic pistol.

On Tuesday morning, September 6, 1949, Freda Unruh made her son a breakfast of fried eggs. But he threatened to smash her head with a wrench, and she fled to the home of a friend. Soon afterward, at about 9:20, Howard Unruh emerged onto the sidewalk of 32nd Street, looking dapper in a brown suit, pressed white shirt, and bow tie. He turned the corner at the Cohens' pharmacy and strolled down River Road.

Unruh passed a couple storefronts before entering the shoe-repair shop of John Pilarchik, one of the people on his death list. The 27-year-old Pilarchik—who like Unruh was a World War II veteran—stared in astonishment as Unruh raised his Luger and, after a fraught moment, squeezed the trigger. The bullet tore into Pilarchik's chest. He staggered and fell, but was still alive when Unruh fired a second round into his head.

Pilarchik's killing marked the start of a 20-minute rampage. The precise sequence is impossible to ascertain.

Eyewitness accounts would vary—which isn't surprising, given the havoc Unruh wreaked. While he may have started out intending to shoot only the handful of people on his death list, he quickly lapsed into indiscriminate killing. His movements, too, were desultory: he wandered south on the tiny block, moved north toward 32nd Street, turned south again. He crossed the street a couple times.

According to Unruh, he went next door, to the barbershop of Clark Hoover, immediately after shooting Pilarchik. "I've got something for you, Clarkie," Unruh announced. Hoover was on Unruh's death list, but the little boy sitting on the hobbyhorse was not. Nevertheless, Unruh pumped bullets into the chest and head of six-year-old Orris Smith—who was getting a trim in preparation for his first day of school—before turning the Luger on Hoover. Catherine Smith, Orris's mother, was screaming hysterically, yet Unruh took no apparent notice. He ambled out of the barbershop without shooting her or two other patrons.

Unruh fired a couple rounds into a small restaurant as he strolled up the block toward 32nd Street. "Children screamed as they tumbled over one another to get out of his way," wrote *New York Times* reporter Meyer Berger, who interviewed more than 50 witnesses after Unruh's rampage. "Men and women dodged into open shops, the women shrill with panic, men hoarse with fear. No one could quite understand for a time what had been loosed in the block."

Amid the pandemonium, according to witnesses, Unruh displayed a preternatural calmness. His step appeared unhurried. He showed no signs of agitation.

Tavern owner Frank Engel locked the doors of his establishment as Unruh approached. Patrons huddled behind the bar. Unruh fired into the tavern but didn't hit anyone.

Frank Engel had grabbed a pistol he owned and climbed to the second floor of the tavern building. Leaning out a window, Engel fired at the gunman on the street below. The bullet struck Unruh in the left thigh, but he seemed not to notice. After the slightest hesitation, he kept walking. He never turned toward Engel.

From inside the River Road Pharmacy, an insurance salesman named Jason Hutton heard the commotion and decided to investigate. He opened the door to find a gunman only a few feet away. "Excuse me, sir," Unruh said, in an incongruous display of politeness. Hutton was too stunned to move out of the way. After a few moments, Unruh shot him dead, stepped over the body, and entered the pharmacy in pursuit of his intended quarry.

Maurice Cohen shouted for his family to hide as he raced upstairs. Cohen scrambled out a window onto the porch roof at the rear of the building. Before the pharmacist could jump, however, Unruh shot him in the back, sending him tumbling off the roof. In the Cohens' living quarters, Unruh saw Rose duck into a closet. He fired a couple rounds through the closet door, then opened it and dispatched Rose with a bullet to the face. Minnie Cohen, Maurice's mother, was in a bedroom trying to telephone the police when Unruh cut her down with his Luger. Unruh left without finding 12-year-old Charles Cohen, whose trumpet practicing had annoyed him. The boy was in a closet. Outside, Maurice Cohen had managed to crawl a few feet down 32nd Street before expiring.

Television repairman Alvin Day probably had no inkling that anything was amiss when he pulled onto River Road. Unruh fired a single shot through the window of Day's truck as it passed. The 24-year-old slumped, lifeless, against the steering wheel as the vehicle came to a halt in front of the River Road Pharmacy.

Down River Road, two doors past Clark Hoover's barbershop, was a tailor shop. Unruh went there to kill the owner, Thomas Zegrino. But Zegrino had gone out on an errand, leaving his wife of one month, Helga, to assist customers. She was hiding at the back of the store. Unruh shot her dead and walked out.

In a nearby apartment, a toddler in his playpen was jiggling some window blinds. Unruh saw movement at the window and fired, hitting Tommy Hamilton in the forehead. The two-year-old died instantly.

Meanwhile, three friends driving down the street had noticed the body of Jason Hutton outside the River Road Pharmacy. The young men stopped to render aid. Unruh spotted the Good Samaritans and fired, hitting 18-year-old Charles Petersen in the legs. Petersen's friends ran away.

As the rampage unfolded, many people found refuge in the small grocery store opposite the Cohens' pharmacy. Unruh went there but found the doors locked. He stood in front of the store for a few moments, then fired a couple of rounds into the building before moving on.

A car was stopped at a red light at the intersection of 32nd and River Road. Unruh strode up to the vehicle and shot the driver, 37-year-old Helen Wilson; her 9-year-old son, John; and her mother, Emma Matlack, 68. The women died at the scene. John Wilson would succumb the following day at the hospital.

Unruh walked down 32nd Street, allowing two women and their young

Police overpower Howard Unruh outside his Camden home.

Howard Unruh is captured by police at the end of his murderous rampage, September 6, 1949.

children to pass unmolested. He broke into a house behind his mother's apartment. There he shot Madeline Harrie, 36, and her 16-year-old son, Armand, before running out of ammunition. Of the 16 people Unruh shot during his rampage, only the Harries and Charles Petersen would survive.

Unruh returned to his mother's apartment. He had no time to collect more bullets and resume his killing spree. Squad cars, their sirens screaming, were converging from every direction. Within minutes, 50 Camden policemen had the building surrounded. They unleashed a barrage of gunfire through the windows and into the apartment.

Soon Unruh's telephone rang. Philip W. Buxton, an assistant editor with the *Camden Courier-Post*, had looked up the number in the phone book, though he didn't really expect anyone to answer his call. To Buxton's surprise, Unruh picked up, sounding calm. After establishing whom he was speaking with, Buxton asked Unruh how many people he had killed.

"I don't know," Unruh replied. "I haven't counted them yet, but it looks like a pretty good score."

Buxton asked why Unruh was killing people. "I can't answer that yet. I'm too busy," Unruh responded. "I'll have to talk to you later. A couple of friends are coming to get me." Unruh hung up the phone.

The police had tossed several tear-gas canisters into the apartment. Minutes later, Unruh surrendered.

"What's the matter with you?" a cop demanded as the suspect was led away. "You a psycho?"

"I'm no psycho," Unruh insisted. "I have a good mind."

Police took Unruh to the Detective Bureau at Camden City Hall. There, he was interrogated by police detectives and Camden County prosecutor Mitchell Cohen. Unruh cooperated fully, though he couldn't recall some details of his shooting spree. His questioners were struck by the matter-of-fact way Unruh described killing neighbors and strangers alike. He seemed untroubled by what he'd done, though he did concede that he deserved whatever punishment might be meted out.

The questioning lasted about two hours. At its conclusion, when Unruh stood up, someone noticed a pool of blood on his chair. Only then did police realize Unruh had been shot. He was taken to Cooper Hospital for treatment.

The following day, Cohen questioned Unruh further in his hospital room. Unruh continued to display a remarkable absence of remorse. He was indicted on 13 counts of homicide and three counts of aggravated assault.

However, psychiatrists hadn't yet determined whether Unruh was mentally competent to stand trial. The psychiatric evaluation would ultimately take a month.

In the meantime, the story of the veteran's rampage—which the media dubbed the "walk of death"—gripped the entire country. America had never before seen this kind of random slaughter by a berserk gunman.

On October 7, 1949, the findings of the psychiatric evaluation were finally announced. Diagnosed with paranoid schizophrenia, Unruh was judged not competent to stand trial. He was instead committed to the Vroom Building for the criminally insane at the Trenton Psychiatric Hospital.

Unruh remained in that maximum-security setting until 1993, when he was transferred to a geriatric unit at the Trenton Psychiatric Hospital. He died in October 2009—60 years after his 20-minute spree shattered a quiet city block and claimed 13 lives.

CHARLES WHITMAN
THE TEXAS TOWER SNIPER

"I don't quite understand what compels me to type this letter," Charles Whitman wrote on the night of July 31, 1966. "Perhaps it is to leave some vague reasons for the actions I have recently performed. I don't really understand myself these days. I am supposed to be an average reasonable and intelligent young man. However, lately (I can't recall when it started) I have been a victim of many unusual and irrational thoughts."

Few who knew Whitman saw any signs of this inner turmoil. In fact, the 25-year-old seemed affable and well adjusted.

His background suggested the ideal of the all-American boy. He'd been an altar boy, an Eagle Scout at the age of 12, and a U.S. Marine. He had an attractive young wife. He was pursuing a degree in architectural engineering. Despite his studies and the part-time jobs he held to put himself through school, he found time to volunteer as a Scout leader. He seemed to have a bright future.

But Whitman had decided that neither he, nor the people he claimed to love the most, nor an unknown number of random strangers were going to have a future. "It was after much thought that I decided to kill my wife, Kathy, after I pick her up from work at the telephone company," he noted in his July 31 letter.

> I love her dearly, and she has been as fine a wife to me as any man could ever hope to have. I cannot rationaly [sic] pinpoint any specific reason for doing this. I don't know whether it is selfishness, or if I don't want her to have to face the embrassment [sic] my actions would surely cause her. At this time, though, the prominent reason in my mind is that I truly do not consider this world worth living in, and am prepared

Case File

Charles Joseph Whitman

Born: *June 24, 1941*

Date of killings: *Aug. 1, 1966*

Location: *Austin, Texas*

Number of victims: *13 killed, 31 wounded on University of Texas campus; 2 killed elsewhere*

Weapon: *Universal M1 semiautomatic .30-caliber carbine; Remington 700 ADL rifle; Remington Model 141 rifle; 12-gauge semiautomatic shotgun; Luger P08 semiautomatic 9-mm pistol; Galesi-Brescia .25 semiautomatic pistol; Smith and Wesson .357 Magnum revolver*

Outcome of case: *perpetrator killed at scene*

Died: *Aug. 1, 1966*

to die, and I do not want to leave her to suffer alone in it. I intend to kill her as painlessly as possible.

Similar reasons provoked me to take my mother's life also.

Whitman's slaying of his wife and mother would be the prelude to one of the most infamous shooting sprees in American history. For about an hour and a half, it transformed the campus of the University of Texas into a veritable war zone.

Charles Joseph Whitman, the eldest of three sons of Margaret and Charles Adolphus Whitman, was born in Lake Worth, Florida, in 1941. His father owned a successful plumbing-supply business, and young Charles grew up amid substantial wealth. He seemed driven to excel in whatever endeavor he undertook: academics, music, the Boy Scouts. He became an expert marksman under the tutelage of his father, a gun enthusiast and avid hunter.

But Whitman, by his later admission, hated and feared his father. Charles Adolphus Whitman, who had a violent temper, physically abused his wife. He also punished his sons harshly if they failed to measure up to the high standards he set for them. In June 1959, around the time of his graduation from high school, Whitman returned home drunk after a night of celebrating with friends. He nearly drowned after his father beat him severely and threw him in the swimming pool.

A month later, determined to get away from his father, Whitman enlisted in the U.S. Marine Corps. After basic training and an 18-month posting to Guantánamo Bay, Cuba, Whitman applied for and received a scholarship that would allow him to obtain a college degree and become a commissioned officer in the Marine Corps. He enrolled in the University of Texas to study engineering.

Charles J. Whitman (dark suit, center) is pictured with his parents and younger brothers John and Patrick. Whitman's disagreements with his father left the young man emotionally drained.

It was there, in 1962, that Whitman met Kathleen Leissner. The 18-year-old Texas native, daughter of a beauty queen, was studying education. Smitten, Whitman dated Leissner for just five months before proposing. In August 1962, the couple married.

Whitman's studies had taken a backseat to romance, and his lackluster grades caused the Marine Corps to revoke his scholarship. In February 1963 he was called back to active duty and ordered to report to Camp Lejeune, North Carolina.

In a diary, Whitman would express his anger toward the Marine Corps. He also deeply missed his wife, who remained in Austin pursuing her degree. After committing a string of relatively minor violations at Camp Lejeune, Whitman was court-martialed in November 1963. He received 30 days' confinement and 90 days at hard labor and was demoted from lance corporal to private. Still, he

Charles and Kathleen Whitman leave St. Michael's Catholic Church in Needville, Texas, after their August 17, 1962, marriage ceremony.

received an honorable discharge from the Marine Corps a year later.

Whitman returned to Austin, where he enrolled once again at the University of Texas. This time he brought intense discipline and focus to his studies, and he earned good grades. Still, his diary entries suggest that he wasn't entirely happy with himself. Though he worked hard at part-time jobs, Kathleen—who had graduated and landed a position

teaching biology at a local high school— was the main breadwinner for the household. Whitman faulted himself for falling short as a provider. In another major blow to his pride, he accepted money from his father to help make ends meet.

Though he despised his father, Whitman had discovered that he was like the old man in at least one respect. On three occasions, as he confided to friends, he'd lost his temper and struck his wife. He was mortified by this and included constant reminders in his diary about how a compassionate and caring husband should act.

In early 1966, Margaret Whitman decided she'd had enough of her own husband's abuse. She moved to Austin to live near her eldest son and soon filed for divorce. Whitman's distraught father began calling him constantly. He asked for his son's help in persuading Margaret to return to Florida and give him another chance. Whitman didn't want to do this, but he didn't want his father to cut off the money he was sending either. Whitman found the entire situation emotionally draining.

Adding to his anxieties, he was taking a heavy course load. Between academics, a part-time job, and family commitments, he didn't seem to have enough time to do everything he believed he needed to do. He began abusing amphetamines for a bit of extra energy. He experienced severe headaches.

Kathleen, noting the stress her husband was under and concerned about his health, suggested that he see a doctor. He agreed. The doctor prescribed the sedative drug Valium and referred Whitman to Dr. Maurice Dean Heatly, staff psychiatrist at the University of Texas Student Health Center.

Whitman met with Dr. Heatly for about an hour on March 29, 1966. In his notes, Heatly recorded that the young man "seemed to be oozing with hostility." The psychiatrist believed that Whitman was distressed over his parents' recent separation, for which he blamed his father. Whitman admitted that his father, despicable though he might be, had achieved much in life, whereas Whitman himself had not. Heatly recognized that this was causing the young man considerable anguish.

During his session with the psychiatrist, Whitman said that something strange seemed to be happening to him; he didn't feel like himself. He confessed that he often thought "about going up on the Tower with a deer rifle and shooting people." The Tower to which Whitman referred was the 307-foot-tall Main Building, designed as the central library for the University of Texas. Since its opening in 1937, the 28-floor limestone structure had dominated the Austin campus. During his years at the university, Dr. Heatly had heard numerous stu-

dents talk about throwing themselves off the Tower. But invariably such talk turned out to be nothing more than idle fantasies borne of the routine frustrations and stresses many college students experience. Heatly didn't read anything much into Charles Whitman's thoughts of taking to the Tower with a deer rifle, beyond the fact the Whitman was mildly depressed. He didn't think Whitman was dangerous. He asked the young man to return the following week or to call anytime he felt the need to talk.

Whitman didn't return to see the psychiatrist the following week. Nor did he ever call. But his diary indicates that he continued to struggle with feelings of inadequacy and anger. No one, not even his wife, understood that he was descending toward homicidal violence.

On the night of July 31, after he'd begun typing the note that he hoped might explain the actions he was about to undertake, Whitman was interrupted by an unexpected visit from friends. Larry and Eileen Fuess found Whitman in good spirits. The three chatted for a while and went out to get ice cream before the Fuesses departed around 8:30 PM. Soon afterward, Whitman left to pick up his wife from her summer job as a telephone operator.

Whitman waited until Kathleen had gone to bed, then drove to his mother's apartment sometime after midnight. He stabbed his mother in the heart with a hunting knife, placing the body on her bed and covering it with a sheet. Then he composed a note in which he insisted that he'd loved his mother very much and that he was sure she was now in heaven, if indeed heaven existed.

Whitman left his mother's apartment around 2 AM and returned to his own home. He stabbed his wife to death as she slept, pulled the sheet over her body, and resumed the note he'd started the previous evening. He didn't bother to type now, but handwrote in blue ink, "8-1-66. Mon. 3:00 A.M. Both Dead." Whitman further attempted to explain his actions, wrote separate notes to his brothers and his father, and issued instructions for disposing of his belongings. He also asked that doctors perform an autopsy to determine whether, as he suspected, his murderous thoughts and actions were attributable to something wrong with his brain.

Whitman had a busy morning on August 1. He called his wife's employer, explaining she was sick and wouldn't be at work that day. He did the same with his mother's employer. He went to the bank and cashed some checks. He visited three stores to buy a carbine, a shotgun, ammunition, and magazines. He rented a hand truck to haul his old marine footlocker.

Back at his house, Whitman sawed off part of the barrel and stock of his new shotgun. He put that weapon, his new carbine, another rifle, and three handguns into his footlocker, along with 1,200 rounds of ammunition. He also packed knives, a machete, a hatchet, food, water, a radio, a flashlight, and other supplies he might need in the event of a long siege. Around 11 AM he drove to campus, parked his car, and wheeled his footlocker to the Main Building on the rented hand truck. Dressed in blue coveralls, he looked like a janitor.

Whitman rode the elevator to the 27th floor of the Tower. He hauled his footlocker up the three flights of stairs to the 28th floor, which offered access to the Tower's famous outdoor observation deck, a popular spot for sightseers. Edna Townsley was on duty inside the 28th-floor reception area. Instead of signing in at her desk, Whitman smashed the 51-year-old in the face with the butt of one of his rifles and delivered another blow after she'd fallen to the floor. He dragged Townsley's body behind a couch.

Presently a couple came inside from the observation deck. "Hi, how are you?" Whitman asked breezily. The couple assumed the gun he was holding was for the purpose of shooting pigeons. They said hello and disappeared down the stairwell to the 27th floor.

Whitman put a desk atop the last flight of stairs, right in front of the door opening to the 28th-floor reception area. But soon two teenaged boys—who were touring the Tower with their parents and an aunt and uncle—slipped past the makeshift barricade and pushed open the door. Whitman unleashed a shotgun blast that sent both boys tumbling down the stairs. One of them was killed instantly, the other critically wounded. Whitman fired down the stairwell at least two more times, seriously wounding the boys' mother and killing their aunt. Then he restored his barricade, fired a round into the back of Edna Townsley's head, and walked out the door onto the observation deck.

Whitman jammed his hand truck against the door and proceeded to unpack his footlocker. He positioned supplies around the 200-foot perimeter of the observation deck. At about 11:48 AM, he stared through the 4X scope of his Remington 700 rifle and fired at a visibly pregnant woman walking near the South Mall. The shot tore through the abdomen of 18-year-old Claire

Smoke rises from Whitman's gun as he fires from the University of Texas tower.

Charlotte Darehshori cowers in fear behind the base of a flagpole while a wounded student lies a few feet away during Whitman's shooting spree.

Wilson, instantly killing her fetus. As Wilson fell to the ground, her fiancé, 18-year-old Thomas Eckman, bent down to help her. He'd barely had time to ask what was the matter before Whitman's second shot entered his shoulder just below the neck. Eckman fell dead on top of his stricken girlfriend.

Initially, nobody on the ground recognized the unusual snapping sounds as the report of a rifle. Many people assumed they were hearing construction noise. But as a half dozen victims fell in rapid succession on the South Mall, a pair of students realized that a gunman was firing from the Tower. The students dove behind a wall and shouted for others to take cover.

Not everyone heard or understood the warning. More people were cut down as they blithely went about their business, unaware of any danger.

Charlotte Darehshori was looking at the South Mall from a window in the office of the dean of the graduate school, where she'd recently been hired as a secretary. Darehshori saw three people fall and rushed out of the building to help them. But when she reached the closest victim, a wounded student, she heard bullets landing all around her and retreated behind the concrete base of a flagpole. She would kneel there for the next 90 minutes, with the wounded student only feet away. "This boy kept looking at me and I couldn't help him," Darehshori recalled.

Whitman soon turned his attention to the west, toward Guadalupe Street. He killed two students trying to hide behind a construction barrier there and wounded another. He killed one of the first police officers to respond to the shooting, 22-year-old patrolman Billy Speed.

Arriving officers immediately recognized that their service revolvers were useless against a gunman firing a high-powered rifle from atop the Tower. Instead of waiting for Austin Police Department headquarters to send the necessary firepower, some officers raced home and grabbed their personal hunting or target rifles. Back at the campus, they were joined by armed civilians.

By about 12:10, the observation deck was being peppered by gunfire. Thereafter, Whitman resorted mostly to shooting through waterspout openings in the deck's walls, which greatly reduced his field of fire. Although the standoff would last another hour and a quarter, most of Whitman's victims had already been hit.

While police and civilians kept Whitman pinned down from below, the Austin Police Department sent a sharpshooter toward the Tower in a small plane. The sharpshooter was unable to get a shot, but Whitman fired a round into the aircraft, causing the pilot to fly out to a safer distance.

Meanwhile, a handful of Austin police officers had entered the Main Building. After the 27th floor was cleared and the wounded evacuated, officers Jerry Day, Ramiro Martinez, and Houston McCoy carefully made their way up the stairs to the reception area of the observation deck. They were joined by Allen Crum, a civilian the officers mistook for a member of campus security. Crum was a former tail gunner in the air force.

Inside the reception area, the men couldn't see the shooter through any of the windows. Martinez tried to open the door to the observation deck quietly. But finding it wedged shut with Whitman's hand truck, he kicked the door open and leaped out onto the south deck near the east corner. The gunman, fortunately, wasn't on that side of the building. Martinez's companions followed him out the door.

The men split up, Martinez and McCoy crawling northward along the east deck, and Day and Crum inching

The body of Charles Whitman lies on the observation deck of the university tower after he was killed by police.

westward along the south deck. As Crum crawled around the southwest corner, he accidentally discharged his rifle. That turned out to be serendipitous, as Whitman positioned himself at the northwest corner and was looking in the direction the blast had originated when Martinez turned the northeast corner. From 50 feet away, the officer fired six shots from his revolver. Apparently, none found their target. Before Whitman could swing his rifle around and return fire, however, McCoy had unleashed two shotgun rounds. They hit Whitman in the head.

At 1:24 PM, after more than an hour and a half, the Tower sniper had finally been stopped. Whitman had claimed the lives of 13, in addition to his mother and wife. He'd wounded 31.

A few days later, as Whitman had wanted, doctors performed an autopsy on his body. They discovered a particularly aggressive brain tumor called a glioblastoma. It would have killed Whitman within months. Whether the tumor could have been responsible for Whitman's violent behavior is difficult to say with certainty, but most brain specialists are doubtful.

For his part Gary Lavergne, who wrote a well-received 1997 account of the Tower massacre, offers a different explanation for what drove Whitman to murder. "Charles Whitman became a killer because he did not respect or admire himself," Lavergne says. "He knew that in many ways he was nearly everything he despised in others, and he decided that he could not persevere. He climbed the Tower because he wanted to die in a big way; not by suicide, but by taking others with him and making the headlines."

RiCHaRD SPECK
TERROR aND MURDER iN CHiCaGO

One day a sparrow flew into Richard Speck's cell at Stateville Correctional Center. Speck—who was serving a life sentence at the maximum-security prison near Joliet, Illinois—caught the bird and, over the course of several weeks, tamed it. He tied a string to the sparrow's leg and carried the bird around on his shoulder.

But this would be no "Birdman of Alcatraz" sort of story, in which the hardened criminal finds a measure of redemption in his nurturing of birds. A Stateville guard told Speck that prison rules prohibited the keeping of pets. He threatened Speck with solitary confinement unless he got rid of the sparrow. Speck didn't set the bird free. Instead he shoved it into a whirring ventilation fan. The sparrow was annihilated in an explosion of feathers. Shocked, the guard said he thought Speck had liked his pet. "I did," the prisoner reportedly responded, "but if it ain't mine, it ain't nobody's." It was the kind of mindless disregard for life that Speck habitually displayed—and that he took to horrific extremes one summer night in 1966.

Richard Speck was born in Kirkwood, Illinois, in 1941. His father died of a heart attack six years later, leaving behind a widow and eight children. Mary Speck remarried in 1950. She and her two youngest children, Richard and Carolyn, settled in Texas with her new husband, an insurance salesman named Carl Lindberg. After a year in the small rural town of Santo, the family moved to Dallas, where Richard Speck would spend the next 15 years of his life—that is, when he wasn't behind bars.

Speck never got along with his stepfather, a heavy drinker who had periodic scrapes with the law and who proved

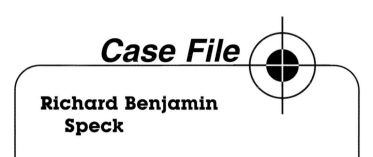

Case File

Richard Benjamin Speck

Born: *Dec. 6, 1941*

Date of killings: *July 14, 1966*

Location: *Chicago*

Number of victims: *8*

Weapon: *knife*

Outcome of case: *convicted of eight homicides, and sentenced to death, in 1967; sentence changed to eight life terms in 1972*

Died: *Dec. 5, 1991*

feckless when it came to providing for his family. Yet Speck would display some of the same shortcomings—in spades. He notched his first arrest at the age of 13 and accumulated more than 40 additional arrests in the decade that followed. He dropped out of school at 16, before finishing the ninth grade. He got drunk almost daily. In 1962, when he was 21, Speck married a 15-year-old he'd gotten pregnant. But when their daughter was born, Speck's wife had no clue as to his whereabouts. He was, she would discover only later, in a county jail serving a three-week sentence for instigating a drunken brawl.

Speck would soon go away for a longer period. Between September 1963 and January 1965, he served 16 months of a three-year sentence for burglary and forgery. Just a week after being released on parole from the Texas State Penitentiary in Huntsville, Speck was back in trouble. He attacked a woman with a knife. That assault landed him in Huntsville for another six months.

In January 1966 Speck's wife filed for divorce. Two months later, in March, he burglarized a grocery store, and a warrant was issued for his arrest. Facing another prison term, Speck fled to Illinois.

In the city of Monmouth, one of his brothers found work for him as a carpenter's assistant. But by mid-April, Monmouth police informed Speck that they wanted to question him in connection with the murder of a barmaid. He abruptly left the hotel where he'd been staying. When police searched his room, they found some jewelry belonging to an elderly woman who'd been raped and robbed several weeks earlier.

Speck ended up in Chicago, where he stayed with his sister's family. Speck's brother-in-law, who had served in the navy, helped him obtain the documents necessary to work as an apprentice seaman in the U.S. Merchant Marine. Speck was hired aboard a freighter plying the Great Lakes. But he soon squandered the opportunity by getting drunk and fighting with one of the ship's officers.

By July Speck's sister and brother-in-law had grown exasperated by his irresponsibility. They had two teenage daughters living at home and thought it best that he find somewhere else to stay. On the morning of July 13, they gave Speck $25 to rent a room. They left him at the National Maritime Union Hall, located in Chicago's South Side at 2335 East 100th Street. The union hall was where merchant sailors in search of work went to find an assignment. A couple days earlier, Speck had thought he'd obtained a job aboard a freighter that was readying to ship out. However, because of a mix-up at the union hall, another sailor had also been recruited for the same position. That man ultimately got the job by virtue of his greater experience. Speck's fury had been wildly disproportionate to the minor setback. And now, two days later,

he continued to simmer. He wasn't in a mood to wait at the union hall for another opportunity. Around noon he gathered his bags and walked about a mile and a half to East Chicago's Shipyard Inn. He registered there for one week.

Speck had a few drinks at the Shipyard Inn's lounge before heading out to sample other bars. After a day's drinking, he returned to his room at the Shipyard Inn with a woman he'd met during his barhopping. He raped her and stole a .22-caliber handgun she had in her purse. Speck released the victim, whereupon he returned to the Shipyard Inn's lounge and resumed his drinking binge.

Sometime after 10:00 PM, Speck left the lounge. He walked to the 2300 block of East 100th Street. A stone's throw away from the National Maritime

Speck tried to find work as a sailor on the freighters that crossed the Great Lakes.

This photo of student nurses at South Chicago Community Hospital was taken in July 1966, just a few days before Richard Speck's deadly attack. Pictured are (left to right) Mary Ann Jordan, Judith Dykton, Suzanne Farris, Nina Jo Schmale, an unknown nurse, and Pamela Wilkening. Speck killed Jordan, Farris, Schmale, and Wilkening; Dykton, who lived across the street, arrived after the killing spree ended and helped the only survivor of the attack, Corazon Amurao, escape from the house.

Union Hall was a row of two-story townhouses, which the South Chicago Community Hospital leased as dormitories for student nurses. Earlier that day, Speck had scoped out the townhouses. What precisely he planned to do is uncertain. He would later say that he intended simply to steal some money, though that claim seems hard to reconcile with his actions.

At about 11:00 PM Speck broke into 2319 East 100th, the unit on the end.

Finding no one on the ground floor, he went upstairs. He tried a bedroom door but it was locked, so he knocked. When Corazon Amurao opened the door, Speck thrust his stolen gun at her. He ordered Amurao and her roommate, Merlita Gargullo, down the hall. In a larger bedroom, three more women—Pamela Wilkening, Patricia Matusek, and Valentina Pasion—were asleep. Speck woke them. Before long Amurao, Gargullo, and Pasion, who were all from the Philippines, scurried into a closet and held the door shut. They came out only after one of their American housemates assured them that the intruder wouldn't hurt them. In the meantime, Speck had pulled Nina Jo Schmale from another bedroom.

Speck turned off the lights and ordered his six captives to sit on the floor. He told them he needed money. One by one, he had them retrieve their purses.

Around 11:45 PM, Speck added another student nurse to his group of prisoners. Gloria Davy had returned to the townhouse from a date with her fiancé.

Speck cut a bedsheet into strips with his pocketknife. He used the strips to bind each woman's hands behind her back and to tie her ankles together. "Don't be afraid," Speck announced reassuringly. "I'm not going to kill you."

Speck placed Davy on a bed and left the other women on the floor. After he'd finished tying up the last of his captives, Speck unbound Wilkening's ankles, yanked her to her feet, and led her out of the bedroom. It was now about 12:30 AM on July 14. Speck took Wilkening to Amurao and Gargullo's bedroom, gagged her, and stabbed her in the heart. From the large bedroom, the other student nurses could hear what sounded like a muffled groan or sigh.

Meanwhile, two more student nurses had arrived. Mary Ann Jordan still lived

with her parents, but she'd planned to stay overnight at the townhouse with her good friend Suzanne Farris, who was engaged to Jordan's brother. Catching a glimpse of the intruder, Farris and Jordan rushed into the large bedroom. But, of course, no one there could help them. Speck burst into the room and, at gunpoint, ordered Farris and Jordan to follow him into the hall. A few moments later, the bound women heard a scream followed by sounds of a struggle—apparently Farris and Jordan saw Wilkening's body and decided to fight. But they proved no match for the knife-wielding Speck. Jordan's body would be found with stab wounds to the chest, neck, and eye. Farris had 18 stab wounds in the back and neck, but Speck ultimately strangled her with a stocking.

About 20 minutes after Farris and Jordan had been taken from the large bedroom, the remaining student nurses heard water running in the bathroom. Speck was washing up. He soon returned to the bedroom and grabbed Schmale. Again, a half hour or so later the sound of running water could be heard. Again, Speck returned to the bedroom to remove another woman.

In the darkness, the terrified student nurses had tried to conceal themselves by wiggling behind a desk or bureau or under a bed. But moving was exceedingly difficult with hands bound tightly behind the back and ankles tied togeth-

A bloodstained floor and dresser in one of the rooms where Speck murdered his victims.

er. Even in the dim light filtering in from the hallway, Speck easily found his captives. At intervals of approximately a half hour, he dragged away Pasion, Gargullo, and Matusek.

Now only Gloria Davy and Corazon Amurao remained. Amurao, a tiny woman just 4 feet 10 inches in height, had managed to wriggle under a bunk bed. But she was sure Speck would be able to spot her. When he returned, however, he went right to the bed where Davy lay. He proceeded to rape Davy, after which he took her out of the bedroom.

Amurao made the gut-wrenching decision to try to inch her way over to another bunk, which had a blanket hanging over the side all the way to the floor. Fortunately for her, Speck was gone for nearly an hour. By the time he returned, Amurao was completely concealed under the bed.

Speck had apparently lost count of how many women he'd killed. He flipped on the lights but didn't search the bedroom. Instead, he collected some coins from the purse of one of his victims, switched off the lights, and left. It was perhaps 3 or 3:30 AM.

Uncertain whether the intruder remained in the townhouse, Amurao didn't dare move from her hiding place. At 5 AM an alarm clock rang, and when no one came to turn it off, Amurao began struggling to loosen her bonds. She was free about a half hour later.

The carnage Amurao saw when she ventured out of the bedroom sent her into shock. There was a body in the bathroom, three in one of the bedrooms, three more in Amurao's own bedroom. Had she gone downstairs, she would have found still another body.

Amurao staggered to her bedroom window and began crying out for help.

No one heard. She pushed the screen out and climbed onto an exterior ledge. "They are all dead. My friends are all dead," she wailed. "Oh God, I'm the only one alive."

Corazon Amurao

Finally a few people heard the young woman's cries. A student nurse who'd gotten up early to study ran over to 2319 and ushered Amurao to her townhouse. A man walking his dog waved down a police car. Soon sirens pierced the stillness of the summer morning. Uniformed police, homicide detectives, coroner's officials, and forensic technicians swarmed to the crime scene.

Even veteran investigators recoiled at what they found inside the townhouse. The eight victims—all between the ages of 20 and 24—had been stabbed, slashed, and strangled. Some showed signs of sexual assault. There was an astounding amount of blood, and much of it hadn't yet dried.

Despite the terror she'd been through, Corazon Amurao was able to provide a good description of the perpetrator: He was a white man with blond hair. He stood about six feet tall. He spoke with a Southern drawl. He had a tattoo on his forearm that said "Born to Raise Hell."

Police escort Richard Speck into the courtroom for his trial in 1967.

Within hours the police had matched that description to a suspect. An attendant at a nearby gas station recalled a tall, blond-haired man with a Southern accent ranting about how he'd lost a shipboard assignment because of a clerical error. The assignments log at the National Maritime Union Hall identi-

fied the aggrieved man as one Richard B. Speck.

While the police zeroed in on him, Speck was thoroughly enjoying himself. Upon leaving the student nurses' townhouse, he'd walked back to the Shipyard Inn and grabbed a few hours of sleep. By midmorning he was spending his victims' money at East Side saloons. After several hours of barhopping, he returned to the Shipyard and began drinking in its lounge. There he received a phone call from his brother-in-law, who told Speck that the union hall had an assignment for him.

In fact, there was no such assignment. A police detective had concocted the ruse before calling the phone number on file for Speck at the union hall, which turned out to be the home phone of Speck's sister and brother-in-law.

Speck called the union hall right after hanging up with his brother-in-law. Unfortunately, the clerk who answered the call wasn't a very practiced liar. When Speck asked which ship the assignment was for, the man faltered, giving the name of a vessel that had sailed a few days earlier. Speck happened to know about the ship in question, and he concluded that the police were looking for him. He promised the clerk that he would be at the union hall within an hour.

Instead he spent the next three days hiding out in the dive bars and flophouses of Chicago's skid row. The murders of the eight student nurses had been all over the news since the morning of July 14. While Corazon Amurao's description of the killer had been disseminated, it wasn't until the 17th—after fingerprints taken from the crime scene were matched to Speck's prints—that the police publicly identified the suspect as Richard Speck. At the Starr Hotel—the 75-cent-per-night flophouse where he was staying—Speck broke a wine bottle and used the jagged glass to slash his wrists. But he didn't have the nerve to see the suicide through to the end. Soon he was bellowing for help. Eventually, someone called an ambulance.

At Cook County Hospital, an emergency room physician cleaned the blood off Speck's arm and saw the tattoo that said "Born to Raise Hell." Recognizing it from newspaper descriptions, the doctor summoned a cop.

Speck told police he couldn't remember killing the student nurses. He said he must have blacked out as a result of alcohol and drugs. The claim was false—Speck had confessed to the ER doctor who treated him at Cook County Hospital. However, that admission couldn't be used in court, as Speck had been given a sedative at the hospital.

Because of the immense publicity surrounding the case, Speck's trial was moved from Chicago to Peoria, Illinois. Corazon Amurao, the prosecution's star witness, identified Speck and riveted the courtroom with a detailed account of how the horrific events had unfolded. Speck's lawyer tried to convince the jury that his client was a victim of mistaken identity, but he couldn't shake Amurao's certitude that Speck was the man who had slaughtered eight of her classmates. The fingerprint evidence against Speck was also damning. On April 15, 1967, after deliberating less than 50 minutes, the jury found Speck guilty of the eight murders. He was sentenced to death.

In 1972, after the United States Supreme Court's *Furman v. Georgia* decision invalidated death penalty laws as they currently existed, Speck was resentenced. He received a life term for each of the eight murders.

Speck died of a heart attack on December 5, 1991. But the notorious killer managed to spur outrage five years later, when a videotape made by prisoners at Stateville surfaced. On the tape, which dated to 1988, Speck was seen snorting cocaine and declaring how much fun he had in prison. Asked about the eight young women he'd butchered, Speck simply said, "It just wasn't their night." And then he laughed.

COLIN FERGUSON

THE LONG ISLAND RAIL ROAD SHOOTER

As usual, the 5:33 PM Long Island Rail Road train was crowded as it pulled out of Manhattan's Penn Station, destination Hicksville, on that Tuesday in early December 1993. Passengers settled into routines familiar to rush-hour commuters everywhere. Some flipped through the newspaper. Others opened a book. Still others looked out the window or shut their eyes after a long day at work. Some, no doubt, were thinking about their Hanukkah or Christmas plans.

A man who got on the LIRR train at the Jamaica station in Queens had plans of an entirely different sort. In his duffel bag was a 9-millimeter semiautomatic pistol, four fully loaded 15-round ammunition clips, and more than a hundred rounds of loose ammunition. The man went to the back of the third car and sat down. About 10 minutes later, as the train approached the Merillon Avenue station in Garden City, he stood up. Pulling the pistol from his duffel bag, he walked up the aisle, passed a row of seats, and turned to face the passengers. He raised his gun and fired, first at people in the seat to his right, then at people in the seat to his left. He then moved forward to the next row of seats. The gunman was, in the words of one reporter, "as methodical as if he were taking tickets."

In the packed train car, it took a few moments before everyone understood the significance of the pop-pop-pop sounds coming from the back. But then a woman screamed, "He's got a gun! He's shooting people!" Many terrified passengers scrambled for the front of the train car. Others ducked under their seats. Still others found themselves paralyzed by shock and fear.

After emptying his pistol's 15-round magazine, the shooter reloaded and resumed his rampage. "I have seven kids. Please don't kill me," a man pleaded. The gunman did spare some people, even as he shot others sitting right next to them. His reasons for doing this—if there were, in fact, any reasons—would never be clear.

"I'm going to get you," the shooter announced, over and over, as he made his way forward. The gunman had gone through a second 15-round clip when two men in the pile of passengers at the front of the car noticed that he was reloading. They rushed him and, joined quickly by a third passenger, managed to subdue him. "Oh God, what did I do? What did I do?" the shooter said. "I deserve whatever I get."

The rampage had lasted about three minutes. Six people lay dead or fatally wounded. Seventeen others had gunshot wounds—many of them serious—but would survive. Two people sustained significant injuries in the stampede to the front of the car.

The shooter was a 35-year-old immigrant from Jamaica named Colin Ferguson. In his pocket police found a four-page note that sought to explain his reasons for the rampage. Ferguson's grievances were wide-ranging and bizarre. But running through his note was an unmistakable current of racial animus. He railed, for example, against Asians and "racism by Caucasians and Uncle Tom Negroes," and he decried "the false allegations against me by the filthy Caucasian racist female on the #1 line."

In the weeks that followed the Long Island Rail Road massacre of December 7, 1993, investigators would discover the shocking depth of Ferguson's hatred toward whites and Asians. He blamed the racism of those groups for his many problems. And, for some time, he had been thinking about retribution.

Commuters bustle on the Long Island Rail Road platform at Pennsylvania Station in Manhattan. This major railroad hub serves 300,000 commuters a day.

Case File

Colin Ferguson

Born: *Jan. 14, 1958*
Date of killings: *Dec. 7, 1993*
Location: *Garden City, NY*
Number of victims: *6 dead,
19 wounded*
Weapon: *Ruger P-89 9mm semiautomatic pistol*
Outcome of case: *convicted of 6
counts of murder, 19 counts of
attempted murder; sentenced to
prison term of 315 years eight
months to life*

Colin Ferguson, one of five sons of Von Herman Ferguson and Mae Ferguson, was born in Kingston, Jamaica, in 1958. The family was wealthy and socially prominent. Von Herman Ferguson was the managing director of a large pharmaceutical company. Colin enjoyed a childhood of privilege. He graduated from one of Jamaica's most prestigious high schools, after which his father got him a job at the pharmaceutical company. He appeared headed for a life of ease. But then, in 1978, Von Herman Ferguson died in a car accident. A short time later, Mae Ferguson was stricken with cancer. She died in 1979.

Although not poor by any means, the Ferguson brothers no longer moved in the same elite social circles they once frequented. In 1982, at the age of 24, Colin Ferguson left Jamaica for the United States. He settled first in Long Beach, California, where he got a job as a clerk at a liquor store. His boss recalled Ferguson as arrogant and standoffish, a person who continually made it clear that he believed he was too good for menial work. Another supervisor noted how easily Ferguson took offense. He often misconstrued routine interactions as insults directed at him. He seemed especially angry at what he perceived as the racist attitudes of whites.

Ferguson eventually left his liquor store job without giving notice. He made his way east, where in 1986 he married. He and his wife rented a home in Westbury, Long Island.

While working at a succession of low-paying jobs, Ferguson enrolled as a part-time student at Nassau Community College during the spring semester of 1987. A school disciplinary board expelled him from one of his classes because of his aggressive behavior toward the teacher.

Ferguson's aggressive behavior was not limited to school. On several occasions Westbury police answered domestic-disturbance calls at the Fergusons' home. By late 1987, Ferguson had moved out of the house, and his wife obtained a divorce in May 1988.

Shortly after the divorce, Ferguson started a job as an office clerk with a home-security company. He held the job for a little over a year, until he fell off a stool and injured his back and neck. Ferguson applied for and received disability payments totaling $300 per month.

He reenrolled at Nassau Community College, where he made the dean's list in three consecutive semesters but had frequent conflicts with professors and fellow students. In the fall of 1990, he transferred to Adelphi University in Garden City as a business administration major. At Adelphi Ferguson's behavior became even more confrontational. He accused classmates and professors of racism, railed against white people, and on a few occasions even hinted at the desirability of getting rid of whites. In one incident, Ferguson claimed that a white woman had hurled racial epithets at him in the school library. Adelphi's director of minority affairs—a history professor who was himself black—was called on to adjudicate the matter. After the professor concluded that the incident hadn't occurred, Ferguson blasted him for betraying black students. Later, Ferguson threatened the professor and was suspended from Adelphi in June 1991. He never returned to the school.

Ferguson was soon embroiled in another dispute, and this time he ended up under arrest. In February 1992, he was riding the subway when a white woman—the "filthy Caucasian racist female" he referenced in the note explaining his shooting spree—sat down in an empty seat next to him. Finding Ferguson encroaching into her seat, and noticing that there was an empty seat on his other side, the woman asked if he would move over a bit. Instead he exploded in rage, cursing at, threatening, and elbowing the woman. At the next stop, she notified police. Ferguson was taken into custody after a scuffle with several officers. The case never went to trial, but Ferguson seethed. He wrote letters to the New York City Transit Authority and to the police commissioner. In them he complained bitterly about the incident, saying he was a victim of vicious, racist treatment.

Ferguson had decided that his disability checks were insufficient. He filed a claim for a lump-sum workers' compensation payment. In September 1992, after several hearings, the New York State Workers' Compensation Board awarded Ferguson more than $26,000. But he soon came to believe that the sum wasn't enough. In April 1993 he applied to have his case reopened.

That same month, Ferguson traveled to California. He checked into a Long Beach motel and applied for a

California driver's license, giving the motel's address as his residence. After receiving the driver's license, Ferguson went to a gun shop, offered the license as proof that he was a California resident, and filled out a form declaring that he didn't have a criminal record. He put a deposit on a Ruger P-89 pistol. Sixteen days later, after the required waiting period for gun purchases in California, Ferguson picked up the Ruger. He returned to New York sometime in May 1993.

Patrick Denis, from whom Ferguson had been renting a small apartment in the East Flatbush section of Brooklyn, noticed a change in his tenant's attitude after his return from California. While Ferguson had long proclaimed his hatred of whites and blamed his problems on white racism, now, Denis thought, he seemed even more paranoid

Before the attack, Ferguson purchased a Ruger P-89 semi-automatic pistol. It had a magazine that could hold 15 bullets.

and less stable. "He talked in the third person about some apocryphal-type doom scenario," Denis said. "He'd quote fiery leaders, twisting it to make it seem like the downtrodden oppressed black people will rise up and strike down their pompous rulers and oppressors."

Meanwhile, Ferguson obsessively pursued his claim for additional workers' compensation. He wrote numerous letters to the Workers' Compensation Board and phoned its offices repeatedly, sometimes two or three times a day. He also hired a law firm to help in his appeal. His persistence appeared to pay off: in September 1993, the Workers' Compensation Board agreed to reopen the case, asking Ferguson to visit a doctor so that the extent of his injuries could be determined. But Ferguson refused to see the doctor, so his case was closed in October. Ferguson faulted everyone involved—from the Workers' Compensation Board to the African-American attorneys working on his behalf—for conspiring against him. He immediately began writing letters to, and calling the office of, New York governor Mario Cuomo. He demanded that Cuomo address the grievous injustice he believed had been done to him.

By late November, Ferguson was planning to take his revenge on white society. On December 7, he bought an eastbound ticket at the Atlantic

Colin Ferguson, wearing a bulletproof vest and surrounded by court officers, arrives at the initial hearing in his case on December 10, 1993.

Terminal in Brooklyn and changed trains at Jamaica Station. As the note he was carrying explained, he deliberately waited until the train was outside New York's city limits before beginning his rampage. This was in deference to New York's African-American mayor, David Dinkins.

Ferguson was indicted on 93 criminal counts in connection with the shooting spree. Two high-profile attorneys, William Kunstler and Ronald Kuby, ulti-

mately agreed to represent him pro bono. They planned to mount an insanity defense. As a black person in the United States, the lawyers would argue, Ferguson had faced constant racism, the cumulative effects of which produced uncontrollable anger and spurred him to murderous violence. This "black rage" legal defense had never before been tried, and it surely would have proved controversial.

In the end, however, Ferguson

Carolyn McCarthy—whose husband, Dennis, was killed in the LIRR massacre and whose son Kevin was seriously wounded—won a seat in the U.S. House of Representatives in 1996. McCarthy, reelected eight times as of 2012, has been a staunch advocate of gun control.

rejected an insanity defense. He fired Kunstler and Kuby and elected to serve as his own legal counsel. He was totally incompetent. Despite the testimony of dozens of prosecution witnesses who identified him as the shooter, Ferguson maintained that he'd fallen asleep on the train during the evening in question. He'd awoken, he said, to find that a white man had stolen his pistol and committed the massacre. Ferguson said all the eyewitnesses who testified otherwise were racists. He failed to call a single witness in his defense. During his closing summation, Ferguson insisted that he was the real victim—that the police, prosecutors, and witnesses had all lied to ruin him. "Vindicate Mr. Ferguson," he asked the jury. "Do not destroy his life more than it has already been destroyed. He has suffered."

Jurors rejected Ferguson's ridiculous arguments. On February 17, 1995, after a two-month trial, they found him guilty. He was sentenced to a prison term of at least 315 years and eight months.

The Long Island Rail Road massacre prompted calls for stricter gun-control laws in the United States. The case helped garner support for the Federal Assault Weapons Ban, which outlawed certain types of semiautomatic firearms and which President Bill Clinton signed into law in September 1994. The law expired in 2004.

THE COLUMBINE KILLERS

ERIC HARRIS and DYLAN KLEBOLD

"Isn't it fun," the young man intones for the video camera, "to get the respect that we're going to deserve?"

"Directors will be fighting over this story," his friend avers. Steven Spielberg? Quentin Tarantino? The youths agree that either of those Hollywood giants might be worthy of bringing their story to the big screen.

The date is March 15, 1999, and Eric Harris and Dylan Klebold are a little more than a month away from staging the event they hope will inspire movies and win them lasting fame. The videotape they are making will explain to the world some details of their "masterpiece."

Harris wants to make sure he and Klebold receive due credit for their originality. They had the idea first, he insists. And, while a few poseurs may have debuted the idea before them, their plan is superior. "I know we're gonna have followers," Klebold boasts, "because we're so . . . godlike. We're not exactly human. We have human bodies, but we've evolved one step above you. . . . We actually have . . . self-awareness."

If Klebold and Harris were discussing, say, a CD their band was recording, or their plans to hack a computer network, then this sort of talk might be dismissed as the bluster of self-absorbed teenagers. But the 17-year-olds were discussing something entirely different. Their "masterpiece" was to be the largest mass murder in U.S. history. For more than a year, the boys had been planning an attack on their high school outside Littleton, Colorado. They hoped to slaughter hundreds of their classmates, teachers, first responders, and even journalists.

In this image taken from one of the videos that the killers made before their Columbine attack, Eric Harris shows off his shooting skills in the Colorado woods.

Eric Harris and Dylan Klebold met in middle school in 1993. Harris was a new kid—his family had just moved to Littleton after his father's retirement from the U.S. Air Force—whereas Klebold had spent his entire life in the Denver area. Neither boy made friends readily. Harris, according to his parents, was content to be by himself; Klebold, by all accounts, was quiet and uncommonly shy. But the two were drawn together. Both were intelligent, gifted students. They had shared interests in baseball and computers.

During their years at Columbine High School, after they'd become best friends, their mutual interests evolved to include industrial music (they both favored the German bands Rammstein and KMFDM); video production; and video games, especially the first-person shooter Doom. Harris and Klebold often went bowling together. They worked at the same pizza parlor. And sometimes they got into trouble together. At the pizza parlor they once set a fire in a sink, which led to Klebold's firing. He was later hired back. At the start of their junior year, the two friends were suspended for hacking into Columbine's computer system to obtain locker combinations.

Like any high school, Columbine—whose total enrollment approached 2,000—had a social pecking order and a variety of cliques. Klebold and Harris were never in the popular crowd, and they certainly endured taunts and snubs at the hands of kids who were. But it's not clear they were relentlessly bullied, as some news reports would later suggest. And by the time they were seniors, the two were themselves known to pick on underclassmen. Klebold and Harris had a circle of friends and seemed to have found a niche. Both worked on Columbine's daily news broadcast, did school video productions, and worked in the computer lab, helping maintain equipment and assisting fellow students with their computer problems.

Yet in their videotapes Klebold and Harris claimed to have suffered constant mistreatment and abuse by their peers. They seemed to resent just about everybody.

In March 1997, Klebold started a journal, which he kept for the next two years. He called it "Existences: A Virtual Book." Its pages, according to forensic psychiatrists and psychologists who examined the journal, reveal a teen

Case File

Eric David Harris

Born: *April 9, 1981*
Died: *April 20, 1999*

Dylan Bennet Klebold

Born: *September 11, 1981*
Died: *April 20, 1999*

Date of killings: *April 20, 1999*
Location: *Columbine, CO*
Number of victims: *13 dead, 21 wounded*
Weapon: *double-barreled shotgun, TEC-9 semiautomatic handgun (Klebold); pump-action shotgun, carbine (Harris); explosives, knives*
Outcome of case: *perpetrators committed suicide at scene of crime*

struggling with depression and alienation. There are multiple mentions of suicide. "Thinking of suicide," Klebold wrote in his first entry, "gives me hope that i'll be in my place wherever i go after this life—that i'll finally not be at war w. myself, the world, the universe." But the journal also records Klebold's infatuation with, and yearning for, a classmate. "I hear the sound of her laugh, I picture her face," he wrote. "I just hope she likes me." Klebold drew pages of hearts in the journal, but apparently he never overcame his shyness and approached the object of his affections. In early November of 1997, he wrote his first journal entry that referenced the possibility of a killing spree.

Harris, meanwhile, had come to the attention of the authorities for his disturbing writings. Early in 1997, he'd had a falling-out with a friend named Brooks Brown, whose car windshield he cracked with a chunk of ice. On several occasions Brown's parents contacted the Jefferson County Sheriff's Department to report incidents of vandalism and phone harassment for which they knew or suspected Harris to be responsible. In August 1997, Brown's parents alerted the sheriff's department to Harris's website. It included obscenity-laced rants against the many types of people Harris hated; boastful accounts of what Harris called "missions"—acts of nighttime vandalism he, Klebold, and another friend had committed; and descriptions of pipe bombs Harris and Klebold had made and, in at least one case, detonated. The sheriff's department, however, failed to investigate.

On the night of January 30, 1998, a Jefferson County sheriff's deputy arrested Harris and Klebold for breaking into a van and stealing electronic equipment. The event seems to have marked a turning point for the boys. They were both accepted into Jefferson County's Juvenile Diversion Program,

which allowed them to avoid prosecution and a criminal record by paying a fine, performing community service, undergoing counseling, and attending anger management classes. But instead of considering themselves fortunate to escape more serious consequences for a felony crime, Harris and Klebold simmered with rage. "Killing enemies, blowing up stuff, killing cops!! My wrath for January's incident will be god-like," Klebold wrote in Harris's 1998 high school yearbook.

That message was written in May, about a month after Harris had started a journal he titled "The Book of God." In it Harris made clear that he saw himself, rather than the van owner, as the aggrieved party in the January arrest. "Isnt america supposed to be the land of the free?" he asked.

> how come If im free, I cant deprive a stupid f---ing dumb---- from his possessions If he leaves them sitting in the front seat of his f---ing van out in plain sight and in the middle of f---ing nowhere on a [Friday] night. NATURAL SELECTION. F---er should be shot.

Harris's feelings of superiority and his contempt for other people spilled forth from virtually every page of his journal. "[N]o one is worthy unless I say they are," he wrote. "I feel like God and I wish I was, having everyone OFFICIALLY lower than me. I already know that I am higher than almost anyone in

Dylan Klebold poses with a TEC-9 semi-automatic handgun, one of the weapons the teenagers purchased illegally in the months before the attack.

[the world] in terms of universal Intelligence." Harris intended to demonstrate his superiority by authoring an apocalyptic massacre at Columbine High. And, a year in advance, he and Dylan Klebold had set the date for that massacre—which they variously referred to as NBK (for *Natural Born Killers*, a favorite movie) or Judgment Day. They would strike in April 1999.

One reason the pair put off their attack for so long was that they wanted to assemble an arsenal of weapons. Their plan, which was conceived by Harris, required more than firearms. In fact, the boys intended to achieve most of the carnage with bombs. Harris even dreamed of using napalm, but he abandoned the idea after several unsuccessful attempts to make jellied gasoline.

By October 1998, Harris had begun building large numbers of pipe bombs.

(Left) Both Harris and Klebold owned several knives, which they carried, but did not use, during the Columbine High School attack.

(Below) The double-barreled, sawed-off shotgun that Dylan Klebold's friend Robyn Anderson purchased at a gun show. This was one of the weapons Klebold carried during the attack.

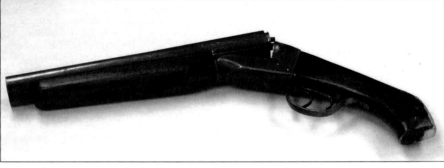

The following month, Harris and Klebold obtained a carbine and two shotguns. As minors, they couldn't legally purchase firearms. But they got Klebold's 18-year-old friend Robyn Anderson to accompany them to a gun show, and she bought the weapons for them. Through Philip Duran, a coworker at the pizza parlor, Klebold and Harris were introduced to Mark Manes, a computer technician who sold them a TEC-9 semiautomatic handgun in January 1999.

One of the tragedies of Columbine is that the massacre might have been prevented. During the many months Harris and Klebold spent preparing for the attack, their plot was nearly uncovered on several occasions. In the spring of 1998, Harris's father found a pipe bomb his son had built. Wayne Harris took away Eric's computer privileges and grounded him for a couple months, but accepted his son's explanation that he'd made the pipe bomb just for fun. Later, Wayne Harris answered a phone call from a clerk at a local gun store, who informed him that the ammunition clips had arrived. Harris told the clerk that he hadn't ordered any clips. Neither man thought to establish whether the clerk had dialed the right phone number and, if so, whether someone else at the Harris residence had placed the ammunition order.

At one point Klebold's parents also came close to stumbling onto the plot. They walked into their son's room while he was trying on a trench coat to see whether it would conceal his sawed-off shotgun. They didn't notice the weapon.

In March 1999, just six weeks before "Judgment Day," Klebold submitted a short story for his creative writing class. Its protagonist, a black-clad gunman armed to the teeth, mercilessly executes a group of "preps" who have wronged him. The teacher found the revenge tale deeply disturbing—she later called it the most vicious thing she'd ever read—but Klebold insisted it was nothing more than a story. In the end, the teacher contacted Klebold's parents but didn't deem it necessary to show them the story.

In retrospect, it's easy to criticize the teacher for not following up more diligently. It's also easy to fault the parents of Dylan Klebold and Eric Harris for missing warning signs of their sons' emotional troubles. And perhaps they should have had some inkling that the boys were planning something terrible. On the other hand, it's undeniable that Harris and Klebold were good at deception. They succeeded in fooling a variety of professionals associated with the Juvenile Diversion Program. They were released from the program a couple months early, and with glowing praise from their case manager. Harris even managed to conceal his smoldering rage from a psychiatrist his parents enlisted to treat their son after his January 1998 arrest. The psychiatrist didn't regard Harris as a danger to himself or others. Harris appeared to delight in his ability to deceive people. "I could convince them that I'm going to climb Mount Everest," he boasted on a videotape, "or I have a twin brother growing out of my back. I can make you believe anything."

Regardless of how skillful Harris and Klebold were at fooling people, competent police work could have foiled their plot. In March 1998, Brooks Brown's parents—who'd learned that Harris was now threatening to kill their son—again brought Harris's website to the attention of the Jefferson County Sheriff's Department. After examining a dozen pages downloaded from the website, investigator Mike Guerra drafted an affidavit for a warrant to search the Harris residence. In the affidavit, Guerra noted that a pipe bomb sheriff's deputies had recovered from a field near Harris's house was consistent with devices the youth described making. Further, Guerra cited specific threats Harris had posted on the website, including a promise to detonate explosives over a wide area and mow down people he hated. "i don't care if I live or die in the shoot out," Guerra reported that Harris had written, "all I want to do is kill and injure as many of you . . . as I can, especially a few people. Like brooks brown." Inexplicably, Guerra's affidavit, prepared in April 1998, was never brought before a judge. Had a search warrant been obtained and executed, it's almost certain that investigators would have found bomb-making materials as well as written evidence of Harris and Klebold's murderous intentions. Instead, the plot went forward.

Like other academically minded high school seniors, Klebold applied to colleges. He was accepted by several and chose the University of Arizona, where he said he would major in computer science. In April 1999 Klebold and his father took a four-day road trip to Tucson so that he could select his freshman dorm. Whether this indicates that

Harris and Klebold wanted to carry out their attack on April 19—the date on which, four years earlier Timothy McVeigh (inset) had detonated a large bomb outside a government office building in Oklahoma City that killed 168 people. But the teens were not ready on the 19th, and had to postpone their attack until the next day.

he was still imagining a life that didn't end in bloodshed, or was simply maintaining a necessary deception, is impossible to say.

For his part, Harris talked to a U.S. Marine Corps recruiter several times during April 1999. But his motivation seems to have been placating his parents, who were concerned about his lack of postgraduation plans. Harris didn't live long enough to find out that the Marine Corps had rejected him because he'd been taking an antidepressant medication prescribed by his psychiatrist.

On Saturday, April 17, Klebold took Robyn Anderson to Columbine High School's senior prom. Harris couldn't find a date but attended the after-party. Classmates would report that both boys seemed in good spirits.

Three days later, Harris and Klebold set out to kill those very classmates. Reporters would make much of the date—April 20, the birthday of Adolf Hitler. While the two friends, especially Harris, did express their admiration for the Nazis, they'd actually intended to carry out their attack on April 19. They'd postponed it only when Mark Manes failed to deliver some ammunition they needed. April 19 was the anniversary of Timothy McVeigh's 1995 bombing of the Alfred P. Murrah Federal Building in Oklahoma City. At the time, that stood as the worst terrorist attack in U.S. history, with 168 dead. In his journal, Harris wrote about exceeding McVeigh's body count.

Around 11:10 on the morning of the 20th, Harris and Klebold arrived at Columbine separately. Klebold parked his car in the senior parking lot, by the school's west entrance. Then he walked over to Harris's car, which was parked in the junior lot, near the south entrance. The boys lugged two large duffel bags, each containing a 20-pound propane bomb, to the school cafeteria. They left the duffel bags and returned to their respective cars, where each boy collected his firearms, donned a black trench coat, and waited.

Three miles to the south, in a park, Harris and Klebold had rigged a massive propane bomb. It was timed to detonate around 11:15. The boys thought the explosion would occupy police, at least for a while, as they attacked Columbine.

The bombs in the school cafeteria were timed to explode at 11:17, when the first lunch period was beginning and, Harris had observed, the cafeteria would be most crowded. The boys believed hundreds of students and staff would be killed by the blast and the resulting collapse of the building. As survivors staggered out of the flaming wreckage, Harris and Klebold would mow them down.

Even with the diversionary bomb in the park, Harris and Klebold expected police to arrive at the school within a few minutes. They also expected to be killed in the ensuing shoot-out. But they'd planned for the carnage to continue even after they were dead. They had rigged their cars with gas containers and bombs set to explode around noon, when the area would be teeming with police, firefighters, paramedics, and TV news crews. The entire spectacle, Harris and Klebold thought, would be like nothing the country had ever witnessed.

But the plan went awry almost from the beginning. Harris hadn't properly wired the bombs, and 11:17 came and went with no explosion in the cafeteria. As the seconds ticked by, students

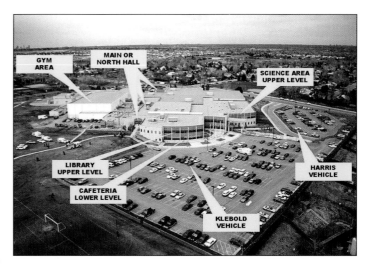

After the attack, the Jefferson County Sheriff's Department produced this aerial photo of Columbine High School, with key areas labeled. The killers' vehicles in the school parking lots had been rigged to explode at noon—a time when Harris and Klebold expected the lots to be filled with students and teachers trying to escape from their bombs and gunfire inside the school.

One of the cafeteria bombs that failed to detonate at 11:17 AM.

began exiting the building and dispersing across the campus. Harris soon made the decision to improvise. He headed over to Klebold's car, and the pair—carrying their guns as well as duffel bags and backpacks full of ammunition, pipe bombs, and Molotov cocktails—then approached the building.

At 11:19 they climbed the outside stairs to the school's west entrance. One of the boys shouted, "Go! Go!" and shots rang out.

In the first minutes of the rampage, Harris fired his carbine repeatedly, targeting anyone within range. By contrast, Klebold largely stood by and watched. Investigators would later find 47 bullets fired by Harris outside the school, whereas only two shotgun

rounds and three 9mm rounds were attributed to Klebold in the initial stage of the attack.

Rachel Scott and Richard Castaldo, both 17, were the first victims. The friends had been eating lunch on the grass near the west entrance to the school. Scott, hit in the head, torso, and leg, was killed. Castaldo would survive eight gunshot wounds but be left paralyzed.

Harris wheeled and fired at three students walking up the stairs. Fifteen-year-old Daniel Rohrbough was killed by a shot to the chest. His two companions were seriously wounded.

Harris and Klebold threw pipe bombs down the stairs, onto the grass, and onto the roof of the building. Harris continued firing at people outside while Klebold walked down the stairs toward the cafeteria.

At first some students in the cafeteria had thought the commotion outside was a senior prank. But teacher Dave Sanders and school custodians Jon Curtis and Jay Gallatine investigated and realized that an actual shooting was under way. They shouted for students to take cover under tables. In the din of the cafeteria, the warnings went unheard until Sanders got students' attention by climbing atop a table. He then dashed up the cafeteria stairs to warn people on the school's second level. Moments later, a stampede began.

Surveillance video shows Harris (left) and Klebold in the cafeteria at Columbine High School during their shooting spree.

A hundred or more panicked students were jammed together on the staircase when Klebold stepped into the cafeteria. He leveled his TEC-9 but didn't fire at the fleeing students. After a few moments, Klebold left the cafeteria and rejoined Harris outside.

The Jefferson County Sheriff's department received the first 911 call from Columbine at 11:23, but there was already an officer on the scene. Deputy Neil Gardner, assigned full time to the high school, had been eating lunch in his patrol car in Clement Park, a few hundred yards northwest of Columbine's campus. The park was where Columbine students went to smoke, and Gardner was watching a group of smokers there when a custodian called him on the school radio with the message that he was urgently needed in the senior parking lot. Gardner

A neighbor took this photo of students fleeing from the high school around 11:35 AM.

flipped on his siren and raced to respond, not yet knowing the nature of the emergency. As soon as he exited his vehicle, Gardner came under fire from Harris, who was about 60 yards away. The officer returned fire, but none of his four shots found their mark.

Harris and Klebold retreated into the second floor of the school via the west entrance. Outside, two classmates were dead and another six lay wounded. Inside, Harris and Klebold tossed pipe bombs. Klebold chased people fleeing down the hallways. After a couple minutes, Harris emerged from the west entrance door to fire at Gardner once again. Another deputy who had arrived on the scene returned fire, and Harris ducked back into the school.

Teachers, meanwhile, were doing their best to get students out of harm's way by leading them out of the building, securing them behind locked and barricaded doors, or directing them to hiding places. Dave Sanders, having instructed the crush of students who followed him up the cafeteria stairs to proceed out the east exits of the school, hustled down a hallway opposite the library. The 47-year-old, who taught business and computers and coached girls' basketball and softball at Columbine, was apparently trying to get other students to safety. From the far end of the hallway, Klebold and Harris spotted him and opened fire. Sanders and a student at his side turned around and ran. The student escaped unharmed; Sanders was cut down just as he rounded the corner. He'd been hit in the neck and back but was still alive. Klebold rushed past him to the top of the cafeteria stairs.

However, the students there had all been evacuated or were hiding, and Klebold returned to the library hallway.

For several minutes, Klebold and Harris walked up and down the deserted hallway. They appeared aimless, firing their guns randomly and throwing pipe bombs at no particular target.

Meanwhile, Sanders managed to crawl to the edge of the nearby science hallway, where another teacher carried him into a biology classroom. There students and teachers tried to staunch the bleeding. A teacher wrote the message "1 BLEEDING TO DEATH" on a whiteboard and placed it in the window. Another teacher, Theresa Miller, called 911. She reported Sanders's condition and provided directions to the classroom. The dispatcher assured her that help was on the way. In fact, it would be hours before help reached the biology classroom.

At about the time Miller first reported that Sanders lay gravely wounded, another teacher was in the midst of a frantic call with another 911 dispatcher. Patti Nielson, who taught art, had been on hall monitor duty when the shooting began. She'd assumed that the racket coming from outside the west entrance was part of a student video production and went to admonish those involved for making too much noise. Harris turned, flashed a smile, and fired his carbine at her. Nielson, wounded slight-

ly in the shoulder, scrambled down the hallway into the library. Believing that the shooter was headed into the school, she shouted for students to hide under tables, ducked behind the library's front counter, and called 911. It was 11:25. The emergency dispatcher told Nielson to stay on the line. Soon Nielson reported that the shooter was in the library hallway. She pleaded for police to be sent. The dispatcher said they were en route. "Oh my God, that was really close!" Nielson exclaimed at 11:29, as blasts of gunfire erupted right outside the library door. Then, a few seconds later, she delivered awful news: "he's in the library, he's shooting at everybody."

By this time, six sheriff's deputies were outside the school. They did not attempt to enter the building.

Three officers from the Jefferson County Sheriff's Department—two lieutenants and a sergeant—would arrive over the next 15 minutes. They set up a command post and made the decision not to send anyone into the school until a SWAT team was ready. Instead, arriving law enforcement personnel—who were converging on Columbine from a host of nearby jurisdictions—were deployed to set up a secure perimeter around the school. Commanders worried that gunmen might slip away into the surrounding neighborhoods, perhaps hidden among a group of fleeing students and staff. Additionally, it was unclear how many gunmen might be involved, with some early reports suggesting as many as eight. The 911 calls, as well as information provided by students and staff who'd gotten out of the building, presented a confusing picture of what was happening inside Columbine High School. Nevertheless, many people would criticize the police for failing to move quickly—particularly after Patti Nielson's 911 call established definitively that people were being shot in the library.

The library became the scene of the worst bloodshed at Columbine. When the killers entered, there were 52 students and four faculty and staff inside. Less than eight minutes later, 10 students would be dead, and 12 others were wounded.

If Klebold had earlier seemed reluctant to participate fully in the attack, by the time the onslaught reached the library, he was acting just as savagely as his partner. After Harris fired his shotgun over the front desk, the pair crossed the room toward the library windows. As he passed Kyle Velasquez, who was mentally disabled and had failed to take cover, Klebold killed the 16-year-old with a bullet to the back of the head. Harris and Klebold then fired out a window at fleeing students and police.

Soon they turned their attention back to the library. They strolled around the room, shooting students cowering under desks and tables. Survivors would say that the killers seemed to be enjoying themselves. They laughed and taunted some of their victims. "Peek-a-boo," Harris said as he bent down to come eye-to-eye with two girls under a table. With a shotgun blast, he killed 17-year-old Cassie Bernall. The recoil slammed the weapon into

An investigator examines bullet damage in the high school library. Harris and Klebold shot 22 students in the library, killing 12.

Harris's face, breaking his nose and leaving him momentarily stunned. This may have saved the life of Bree Pasquale, the girl next to Bernall. As Harris regained his senses, Klebold announced from across the room that he'd discovered a black student, and Harris went to join his partner. The two insulted Isaiah Shoels, one of the few African Americans at Columbine, with racial epithets. Then they fired under the table where the 18-year-old was hiding. Harris killed Shoels with a shot to the chest. Klebold wounded another student who had taken cover under the same table.

At one point, Klebold let an acquaintance of his leave the library. Otherwise, there appeared to be no rhyme or reason to whom the killers passed over and whom they targeted. They had enough ammunition to kill everyone in the library. But after a final salvo under a table killed 17-year-old Corey DePooter and wounded two other students, Harris tossed a Molotov cocktail, and he and Klebold left the library. It was 11:36.

The killers wandered to the science wing. They shot into unlocked and empty rooms, and they taped a bomb to a door. But they made no attempt to enter locked rooms—even, in some cases, after looking through windows and making eye contact with people inside.

The killers proceeded to the cafeteria. A surveillance camera captured Harris firing his carbine from the steps, apparently in an unsuccessful attempt to detonate one of the propane bombs. There were still a few students hiding in the cafeteria, but the killers didn't see them as they walked around the room. Klebold threw a small explosive device toward one of the propane bombs, and at 11:46, as the killers left the cafeteria, a fire broke out. A small explosion followed, but the propane bomb didn't fully detonate, and sprinklers eventually extinguished the blaze.

Harris and Klebold, meanwhile, wandered the upstairs hallways, firing randomly into walls and ceilings as they went. They entered the school office, discharged their weapons, and left. Around 11:56 the killers returned to the

Harris and Klebold shot at this duffel bag in the cafeteria, hoping to detonate the bomb inside.

Powder smoke can be seen as Harris and Klebold shoot from the library windows at deputies and paramedics rescuing the wounded below, between 12:02 and 12:05 PM. Moments later, the two killers took their own lives.

cafeteria. They went to the kitchen area, where 16 students and two members of the school staff had barricaded the door to a storage room. The killers tried to push the door open but quickly gave up.

At noon Harris and Klebold left the cafeteria and went back to the library. With the exception of two seriously wounded students, teacher Patti Nielson, and three staff members and another slightly wounded student locked in closets, all the survivors of the earlier shooting spree in the library had escaped via an emergency exit. Now

Harris and Klebold fired out the windows, and police returned fire. At about 12:08, Nielson heard the killers count to three, and gunshots immediately followed. Harris had ended his life with a shotgun blast through the roof of the mouth, Klebold with a TEC-9 round to the left temple.

Around 12:06 a SWAT team had entered the building through the southeast doors. About an hour later, a second SWAT team broke through the windows of the faculty lounge, near the cafeteria at the school's west end. But the teams, uncertain whether gunmen remained inside the school, proceeded slowly. Room by room, they laboriously cleared the 250,000-square-foot building, searching for gunmen and evacuating the terrified survivors they found.

In the library, 17-year-old Patrick Ireland slipped in and out of consciousness. He'd been shot twice in the head and once in the foot. Somehow Ireland crawled across the library floor to the windows. Two police officers standing on top of an armored car caught the junior as he rolled himself out the second-floor window at 2:38. It would be another 45 minutes before a SWAT team finally reached the library. They were in

time to save the life of Lisa Kreutz, who'd suffered multiple gunshot wounds.

For Dave Sanders, however, help came too late. A SWAT team reached the biology classroom at 2:42. They evacuated students and other teachers, but Sanders bled to death before paramedics could get him out of the building. Among the 13 people killed at Columbine, he was the only teacher and the last to die. Klebold and Harris wounded 21 people in the attack.

The United States had witnessed school shootings in the years before Columbine. In December 1997, for example, a 14-year-old boy had opened

A 14-year-old Columbine High School student hugs her parents after escaping from the massacre on April 20, 1999.

Relatives and community members gather to commemorate the ten-year anniversary of the Columbine High School shootings at the Columbine Memorial Park in Littleton, Colorado, on April 20, 2009. The memorial, which is not far from the school, was dedicated in 2007. Its creators hoped that the memorial "would serve to honor those innocent victims but also provide a historic record of this tragedy and to deliver a message of hope for many generations to come."

fire on a student prayer group at his high school in Paducah, Kentucky, killing three and wounding five. The following March, a pair of boys had murdered four classmates and a teacher at their middle school in Jonesboro, Arkansas. But the Columbine massacre was especially shocking, not only because of the scale of the carnage but also because of the perpetrators' extreme callousness. What could have driven two seemingly normal teenagers to such depths of cruelty?

Based largely on early news reports, many people concluded that the Columbine rampage was retaliation against school bullies, especially jocks. But the evidence doesn't really support that conclusion. During their spree, the killers shot classmates indiscriminately. In the library, where they had everyone trapped, they easily could have separated jocks or bullies or students they didn't like from all the others. Yet they didn't. Even more revealingly, on their videotapes Harris and Klebold acknowledged that their friends might not survive "Judgment Day," but this didn't appear to trouble them in any way.

During the summer of 1999, the FBI began a study of school shootings. Experts who scrutinized the Columbine evidence, particularly the writings and videos left by the killers, would come to a surprising conclusion: Klebold and Harris had strikingly different motives for carrying out the massacre. This reflected enormous differences in their personalities and mental conditions. Klebold, according to the FBI's team of psychiatrists and psychologists, suffered from depression. Harris, by contrast, displayed all the hallmarks of a psychopath. So whereas Klebold struggled with low self-esteem, Harris had grandiose ideas about his own self-worth. Whereas Klebold blamed himself for his problems, Harris rationalized any setback he experienced as the fault of someone else. Klebold, like many depressives, had a great deal of anger, and it often focused outward on other people. Harris wasn't really angry with other people but contemptuous of them. Klebold, the FBI team suggests, saw death as the solution to his emotional misery, and Harris managed to harness and channel that impulse in the service of his own desire to kill unprecedented numbers of people. That act, in Harris's view, would demonstrate his superiority. "Klebold was hurting inside," notes Dwayne Fuselier, the FBI's lead Columbine investigator, in summing up the reason for the massacre, "while Harris wanted to hurt people."

SEUNG-HUI CHO
THE VIRGINIA TECH MASSACRE

In the wake of a mass shooting, one question that inevitably gets asked—after why the perpetrator went berserk—is whether the shooting could have been prevented. Had warning signs been missed? Should someone have been able to discern the perpetrator's sinister intentions?

If the shooter had displayed clear signs of mental illness, many people assume the answer must be yes. But that assumption is dubious at best. Recent studies do show that, compared with the general population, individuals with a severe mental disorder are about twice as likely to commit an act of violence. Yet in absolute terms the risk remains quite small: the overwhelming majority of people with mental illnesses are not violent. In fact, substance abuse, a recent divorce, and unemployment are all stronger predictors of violence than is mental illness.

Patterns of behavior and discrete incidents from a shooter's life often appear to fit neatly into the narrative of a troubled individual moving steadily toward murderous aggression. Of course, that narrative is assembled only after the end point—the rampage—is known. Human behavior is invariably more ambiguous as it is actually playing out. Not even the most experienced psychiatrist or psychologist can say with certainty whether a person who seems to be at risk for violence will actually commit a violent offense. "People exhibit different kinds of behavior or thinking patterns that could possibly lead to a violent act," notes forensic psychiatrist Douglas Mossman. "But the problem is that there are hundreds of individuals who display these same patterns, who don't go on to act violent."

The case of Seung-Hui Cho illustrates this reality. Cho had a long history of mental and emotional problems. Everyone with whom he came into contact could see that he was profoundly maladjusted. A few people found Cho's behavior menacing, but he had no history of actual violence—until he authored America's deadliest school shooting ever.

Cho was born in South Korea in 1984. His family, which included an older sister, immigrated to the United States when he was eight. They eventually settled in Centreville, Virginia.

In South Korea Cho had been quiet and shy. In the United States he appeared even more withdrawn. He had no friends and apparently preferred to spend his time alone. Initially, this was attributed to the language barrier and to difficulty adjusting to a new culture. But even after Cho had been in the country for years and learned English, he con-

tinued to shun contact with other people. Outside of his home, he wouldn't speak, even to say hello to peers or answer a teacher's direct question. But he didn't get into fights or present any disciplinary problems at school.

By middle school Cho had been diagnosed with severe social anxiety disorder. In June 1999 a child psychiatrist performed a thorough evaluation and concluded that Cho suffered from selective mutism—a disorder characterized by an unwillingness to speak in certain social situations—and depression. Cho was prescribed an antidepressant, which he took for a year, until his mood improved.

Throughout high school, however, Cho spoke only reluctantly. He continued to avoid social situations. But with special accommodations, he earned good grades.

Seung-Hui Cho's father earned a modest living by running a small bookstore in Seoul, the capital and largest city in South Korea. The Cho family left South Korea for the United States in 1992. According to relatives, they never returned to visit their homeland.

Cho's guidance counselor strongly recommended that he attend a small college close to home. Instead he chose Virginia Polytechnic Institute and State University, a school with about 25,000 undergraduate students whose Blacksburg campus is 250 miles from Centreville.

In the fall of 2003, Cho entered Virginia Tech as a business information technology major. During his freshman year he did fairly well academically, though he isolated himself socially. Students in his dorm would note that Cho often didn't even acknowledge their presence.

Cho's grades fell markedly during his sophomore year, and he decided to change his major. By the fall of 2005, as his junior year began, Cho was studying English. He wanted to be a writer.

Cho now lived in a four-person suite. His suitemates initially sought to include him in social activities, but he didn't appear interested. At the same time, he exhibited bizarre behavior. He said he had a supermodel girlfriend named Jelly, who called him Spanky and traveled through space to visit him. Cho sometimes phoned his suitemates, identifying himself as "Question Mark" and asking to speak with Cho, his twin brother.

Meanwhile, Cho had become an unsettling presence for at least one of his professors. In a poetry class taught

Case File

Seung-Hui Cho

Born: *Jan. 18, 1984*
Date of killings: *Apr. 16, 2007*
Location: *Blacksburg, Virginia*
Number of victims: *32 killed; 23 wounded or injured*
Weapon: *Walther P22 semiautomatic pistol; Glock 9mm semiautomatic pistol*
Outcome of case: *perpetrator committed suicide at scene*
Died: *Apr. 16, 2007*

by Nikki Giovanni, Cho always hid his features behind dark sunglasses and a baseball cap. Using his cell phone camera, he snapped pictures of female classmates' legs. His writing contained disturbing images and was often overtly hostile. In one paper, titled "So-Called Advanced Creative Writing—Poetry," Cho wrote of his classmates, "I don't know which uncouth, low-life planet you come from but you disgust me. In fact, you all disgust me . . . . I hope y'all burn in hell."

Giovanni asked Cho several times to change his behavior, but he didn't. She told him she believed he'd be better off with a different teacher and offered to help him switch classes. But he balked.

Giovanni thought Cho was trying to intimidate her. "There was something mean about this boy," she would later say. "It was the meanness—I've taught troubled youngsters and crazy people—it was the meanness that bothered me. It was a really mean streak." When other students stopped coming to class because of Cho, Giovanni insisted that he be removed from her class.

Ultimately the head of the English Department, Lucinda Roy, and another professor gave Cho individualized instruction. Roy urged Cho to seek counseling, but he did not.

In late November and early December 2005, three female students reported Cho for harassing them with unwanted phone calls, online messages, or personal contacts. Two of the women called the Virginia Tech Police Department (VTPD). No charges were filed, but Cho's case was referred to university officials for possible disciplinary action.

On December 13, VTPD officers visited Cho and told him to have no further contact with one of the women who'd filed a complaint against him. After the police left, Cho sent an online message to his suitemate. "I might as well kill myself now," it read. The suitemate promptly called the VTPD.

A psychiatrist certified that Cho was an imminent danger to himself or others, and a judge issued an order for his temporary detainment. Cho was taken to Carilion St. Albans Psychiatric Hospital, in nearby Radford, for overnight observation and a full psychiatric evaluation. He was released in the early afternoon on December 14. The psychiatrist who examined Cho wrote that the young man showed "no indication of psychosis, delusions, suicidal or homicidal ideation. . . . His insight and judgment are normal."

Cho was supposed to receive outpatient treatment. He made only one appointment with Virginia Tech's Cook Counseling Center.

During the spring and fall semesters of 2006, several of his professors were alarmed by Cho's strange classroom behavior and violence-infused writing, including a story in which the main character plots to kill students at his school as well as himself. One professor offered to take Cho to counseling, but he demurred. She reported her concerns about Cho to Virginia Tech's associate dean of students. No action was taken, because Cho hadn't made any explicit threats and because the dean was apparently unaware of Cho's contacts with the police or mental health issues.

In February 2007, Cho ordered a semiautomatic pistol online and picked it up at a local gun store. The following month, he bought another semiautomatic pistol from a gun store in Roanoke.

Two background checks had failed to turn up Cho's involuntary (albeit brief) stay at the psychiatric hospital.

Cho stocked up on extra magazines and ammunition for his weapons. He practiced shooting at a pistol range. He videotaped a rambling, incoherent message in which he blamed other people for what he was about to do. "You had 100 billion chances and ways to avoid today," he ranted. "But you decided to spill my blood. You forced me into a corner and gave me only one option. The decision was yours. Now you have blood on your hands that will never wash off." On the morning of Monday, April 16, 2007, he mailed the video, along with photos of himself and a letter, to NBC News.

Around 7:15 AM that same day, Cho fatally shot freshman Emily Hilscher in her dorm room in West Ambler Johnston Hall. Cho also shot and killed resident assistant Ryan C. Clark, 22, whose room was next to Hilscher's. Presumably Clark had heard the gunshots and gone to investigate or to help Hilscher. Cho returned to his suite in Harper Hall, where he changed out of his bloody clothes.

There weren't any eyewitnesses to the shooting. In interviewing people in and around the hall, however, police detectives received what appeared to be significant information. A friend reported that Hilscher's boyfriend, a student at Radford University, usually dropped Hilscher off at the residence hall on Monday mornings. Further, the boyfriend was a gun enthusiast. Police assumed that the shooting had grown out of an argument between the couple. Dozens of officers from the Virginia Tech and Blacksburg police departments scoured the campus in search of

Cho shows off the weapons—a Walther P22 pistol and a Glock 9mm pistol—that he would use to murder more than 30 students at Virginia Tech. This disturbing image was one of several that Cho sent to NBC News before beginning his murder spree.

Hilscher's boyfriend or his pickup truck. When his vehicle wasn't found, the police assumed that he'd left the campus—and hence that there was no further danger to anyone at Virginia Tech.

Between 9:15 and 9:30, Cho entered Norris Hall, a four-story academic building. From the inside, he chained shut the three main entrances to the building.

Cho proceeded to the second floor. Around 9:40 he strode into room 206, where Professor G. V. Loganathan was teaching a graduate engineering class. Chi killed Loganathan and 9 of the 13 students in the classroom. Three other students were wounded.

Next Cho went across the hall, to room 207. He gunned down German instructor Christopher James Bishop and began shooting the students at the front of the classroom. At first sophomore Derek O'Dell couldn't process what was happening. As Cho went about methodically executing his classmates, he made eye contact with the

Candles and flowers were placed on the Virginia Tech campus as a memorial to Seung-Hui Cho's victims.

killer. "That's probably the scariest thing," O'Dell recalled. There was nothing there, just emptiness almost. Like you can look in people's eyes and you can see life, their stories. But his—just emptiness." O'Dell scrambled toward the back of the room and took a bullet in the arm. He lay still, and Cho soon left the room. Two students who hadn't been hit, joined by O'Dell and another wounded student, went to the door and held it shut with their hands and feet.

Jocelyne Couture-Nowak's French class had barricaded the door to room 211 with a desk. But Cho managed to push his way in and continue the slaughter.

Police received the first 911 call at 9:42, and officers were at Norris Hall three minutes later. However, they were unable to get into the building because of the chains on the entrance doors.

Cho, meanwhile, left room 211 and returned to room 207. But the four students holding the door shut prevented him from getting in, so he went back to the French classroom and pumped more bullets into the people there. Only three students who played dead would survive.

Liviu Librescu, an engineering professor, blocked the door to room 204 and shouted for his students to jump out the windows as Cho approached. Firing through the door, Cho killed the 76-year-old Librescu, but 10 of his students managed to escape out the windows. Two others were shot.

At 9:50 police finally gained entrance to Norris Hall through the door to a machine shop. They blasted the lock off with a shotgun. One minute later, just as the police reached the second floor, Cho ended his life with a bullet to the head.

Cho had fired more than 170 rounds in about 11 minutes, and the carnage was appalling: 32 dead, 17 wounded. Six others had been injured while escaping.

In the materials he sent to NBC News, Cho had compared himself to Jesus Christ and to Columbine killers Eric Harris and Dylan Klebold. One of those comparisons was fitting.

CHAPTER NOTES

p. 7: "What is government . . ." Nick Baumann, "Exclusive: Loughner Friend Explains Alleged Gunman's Grudge Against Giffords," *Mother Jones*, January 10, 2011. http://www.motherjones.com/politics/2011/01/jared-lee-loughner-friend-voicemail-phone-message

p. 7: "mind control and brainwash . . ." Suzy Khimm, "Jared Lee Loughner: Meet Rep. Giffords' Alleged Shooter," *Mother Jones*, January 8, 2011. http://www.motherjones.com/mojo/2011/01/jared-lee-loughner-gabrielle-giffords

p. 9: "I never came across one . . ." Associated Press, "Experts Say Mass Murders Are Rare but on Rise," *New York Times*, January 3, 1988.

p. 10: "Before they die . . ." Associated Press, "Many Factors Drive Mass Murders," NBC News.com, April 6, 2009. http://www.msnbc.msn.com/id/30075905/ns/us_news-crime_and_courts/t/experts-many-motives-drive-mass-murders/#.UQcox4sS-Rm

p. 10: "Society had its chance," Harold Schechter, *The Serial Killer Files: The Who, What, Where, How, and Why of the World's Most Terrifying Murderers* (New York: Ballantine Books, 2003), p. 12.

p. 10: "Instead of snapping . . ." Jeffrey Kluger, "Inside a Mass Murderer's Mind," *Time* (April 19, 2007). http://www.time.com/time/magazine/article/0,9171,1612694,00.html

p. 18: "He was working . . ." transcript, NPR Story Corps, "Survivors Recall 1927 Michigan School Massacre," April 17, 2009. http://www.npr.org/templates/transcript/transcript.php?storyId=103186662

p. 19: "After the first shock . . ." Tim Stanley, "Connecticut School Shootings: It's Not Just Guns. America's Attitude to Mental Health Needs Changing Too," *The Telegraph*, December 17, 2012. http://blogs.telegraph.co.uk/news/timstanley/100194499/connecticut-school-shootings-its-not-just-guns-americas-attitude-to-mental-health-needs-changing-too/

p. 20: "There was a pile of children . . ." Monty J. Ellsworth, *The Bath School Disaster* (1927). Text at http://daggy.name/tbsd/tbsd-t.htm

p. 21: "was like speaking . . ." NPR Story Corps, "Survivors Recall 1927 Michigan School Massacre."

p. 21:   "the world's worst demon," Ibid.

p. 22:   "They have been making derogatory . . ." Bruce Shipkowski, "Camden Mass Murderer Howard Unruh Dies at 88," Philly.com, October 20, 2009. http://www.philly.com/philly/news/new_jersey/20091020_Camden_mass_murderer_Howard_Unruh_dies_at_88.html?c=r

p. 23:   "Since he came home . . ." Ibid.

p. 25:   "I've got something . . ." Mara Bovsun, "The Father of Mass Murder," *New York Daily News*, September 6, 2008. http://articles.nydailynews.com/2008-09-06/news/17905961_1_howard-unruh-rose-cohen-bullets

p. 25:   "Children screamed as they tumbled . . ." Meyer Berger, "Veteran Kills 12 in Mad Rampage on Camden Street," *New York Times*, September 7, 1949. http://partners.nytimes.com/library/national/090749nj-shoot.html

p. 25:   "Excuse me, sir," Bovsun, "Father of Mass Murder."

p. 29:   "I don't know. I haven't counted . . ." Ibid.

p. 29:   "What's the matter . . ." Richard Goldstein, "Howard Unruh, 88, Dies; Killed 13 of His Neighbors in Camden in 1949," *New York Times*, October 19, 2009. http://www.nytimes.com/2009/10/20/nyregion/20unruh.html?_r=2&adxnnl=1&pagewanted=all&adxnnlx=1354806559-3CdshTvUfmz1zfKoBG6Q6w&

p. 31:   "I don't quite understand . . ." William J. Hellmer, "The Madman on the Tower," *Texas Monthly* (Aug. 1986), p. 169.

p. 31:   "It was after much thought . . ." Ibid.

p. 35:   "seemed to be oozing . . ." Gary M. Lavergne, *A Sniper in the Tower: The Charles Whitman Murders* (Denton: University of North Texas Press, 1997), p. 70.

p. 35:   "about going up on the Tower . . ." Ibid., p. 71.

p. 36:   "8-1-66 . . ." Hellmer, "Madman on the Tower," p. 169.

p. 36:   "Hi, how are you?" Ibid., p. 167.

p. 39:   "This boy kept looking . . ." "Deranged Tower Sniper Rained Death on UT Campus," *Houston Chronicle*, July 8, 2001. http://www.chron.com/life/article/Deranged-tower-sniper-rained-death-on-UT-campus-2044920.php

p. 40:   "Charles Whitman became a killer . . ." Lavergne, *Sniper in the Tower*, 269.

p. 41:   "I did, but if it ain't . . ." Robert K. Ressler and Tom Schachtman, *Whoever Fights Monsters* (New York: St. Martin's Paperbacks, 1992), 71.

p. 45:   "Don't be afraid . . ." Dennis L. Breo, "July 14, 1966," *Chicago Tribune*, July 8, 2006. http://articles.chicagotribune.com/1986-07-06/features/8602180463_1_student-nurses-bedroom-door

p. 47:   "They are all dead . . ." Bob Secter, "The Richard Speck Case," *Chicago Tribune*, July 19, 2012. http://www.chicagotribune.com/news/politics/chi-chicagodays-richardspeck-story,0,4911196.story

p. 49:   "It just wasn't . . ." Ibid.

p. 50:   "as methodical as if . . ." Francis X. Clines, "Death on the L.I.R.R.: The Rampage; Gunman in a Train Aisle Passes Out Death," *New York Times*, December 9, 1993. http://www.nytimes.com/1993/12/09/nyregion/death-on-the-lirr-the-rampage-gunman-in-a-train-aisle-passes-out-death.html

p. 50:   "He's got a gun! . . ." Ibid.

p. 51:   "I have seven kids . . ." Ibid.

p. 51:   "I'm going to get you," Diana Jean Schemo, "Death on the L.I.R.R.: The Confrontation; 3 Credited in Capture of Gunman," *New York Times*, December 9, 1993.

p. 51:   "Oh God, what . . ." Clines, "The Rampage."

p. 51:   "racism by Caucasians . . ." Charisse Jones, "Death on the L.I.R.R.: The Suspect; In
          Notes and Past of Accused, Portrait of Boiling Resentment," *New York Times*, December
          9, 1993. http://www.nytimes.com/1993/12/09/nyregion/death-lirr-suspect-notes-past-
          accused-portrait-boiling-resentment.html?src=pm

p. 51:   "the false allegations . . ." Richard Perez-Pena, "Woman in '92 Subway Dispute with
          L.I.R.R. Suspect Says All the Signs Were There," *New York Times*, December 13, 1993.

p. 54:   "He talked in the third person . . ." Robert D. McFadden, "A Tormented Life—A Special
          Report; A Long Slide from Privilege Ends in Slaughter on a Train," *New York Times*,
          December 12, 1993. http://www.nytimes.com/1993/12/12/nyregion/tormented-life-spe-
          cial-report-long-slide-privilege-ends-slaughter-train.html?src=pm

p. 56:   "Vindicate Mr. Ferguson . . ." Jere Hester, "Counsel for the Defense: Colin Ferguson
          Goes to Trial, 1995," *New York Daily News*, December 11, 1998. http://articles.nydai-
          lynews.com/1998-12-11/news/18077071_1_colin-ferguson-commuters-long-island-rail-
          road

p. 57:   "Isn't it fun . . ." Nancy Gibbs and Timothy Roche, "The Columbine Tapes," *Time*
          (December 20, 1999). http://www.time.com/time/magazine/article/0,9171,992873-
          1,00.html

p. 57:   "Directors will be fighting . . ." Alan Prendergast, "Hiding in Plain Sight," *Westword*,
          April 13, 2006. http://www.westword.com/2006-04-13/news/hiding-in-plain-sight/

p. 57:   "I know we're gonna . . ." Ibid.

p. 59:   "Thinking of suicide . . ." Dave Cullen, "The Reluctant Killer," *The Guardian*, April 24,
          2009. http://www.guardian.co.uk/world/2009/apr/25/dave-cullen-columbine

p. 59:   "I hear the sound . . ." Kirk Johnson, "Journals Reveal Ruminations of Teenage
          Columbine Killers," *New York Times*, July 7, 2006.
          http://www.nytimes.com/2006/07/07/us/07columbine.html?_r=0

p. 60:   "Killing enemies . . ." CBS News, "The Columbine Shooters."
          http://www.cbsncws.com/2100-270_162-4929050.html

p. 60:   "Isnt america supposed to be . . ." Eric Harris' Journal, at *Columbine Online: Explore a
          Decade of Dave Cullen's Research*. http://columbine-online.com/journals/columbine-eric-
          harris-journal.htm

p. 60:   "[N]o one is worthy . . ." Ibid.

p. 63:   "I could convince them . . ." Prendergast, "Hiding in Plain Sight."

p. 63:   "i don't care if I live . . ." Draft affidavit for search warrant of Harris residence.
          http://dylanklebold.com/documents/73826/search-affidavit.pdf

p. 66:   "Go! Go!" Cullen, "Reluctant Killer."

p. 69:   "Oh my God . . ." Patti Nielson 911 call audio and transcription.
          http://i.a.cnn.net/cnn/SPECIALS/2000/columbine.cd/videos/PATTI.mpg

p. 70:   "Peek-a-boo," Trent Seibert, "Library Killing Rampage Relived," *Denver Post*, May 16,
          2000. http://extras.denverpost.com/news/col0516d.htm

p. 74:   "would serve to honor . . ." Columbine Memorial Foundation, "Overview."
          http://www.columbinememorial.org/Overview.asp

p. 75:   "Klebold was hurting . . ." Dave Cullen, "The Depressive and the Psychopath," *Slate*,
          April 20, 2004. http://www.slate.com/articles/news_and_politics/assessment/2004/04/
          the_depressive_and_the_psychopath.single.html

p. 77:   "People exhibit different . . ." Linda Thrasybule, "Why Mass Killers Aren't Necessarily
          Psychopaths," Yahoo! News, August 13, 2012. http://news.yahoo.com/why-mass-killers-
          arent-necessarily-psychopaths-164158245.html

p. 79: "I don't know which uncouth . . ." Virginia Tech Review Panel, *Mass Shootings at Virginia Tech, April 16, 2007. Report of the Virginia Tech Review Panel*, August 2007, p. 42. http://www.governor.virginia.gov/tempcontent/techPanelReport-docs/FullReport.pdf

p. 80: "There was something mean . . ." Jonathan Pitts, " 'We Are Brave Enough'," *Baltimore Sun*, April 19, 2007. http://articles.baltimoresun.com/2007-04-19/features/0704190025_1_nikki-giovanni-virginia-tech-hokie

p. 80: "I might as well . . ." *Report of the Virginia Tech Review Panel*, 23.

p. 80: "no indication of psychosis . . ." Ibid.

p. 81: "You had 100 billion chances . . ." Emily Friedman, "Va. Tech Shooter Seung-Hui Cho's Mental Health Records Released," ABC News, August 19, 2009. http://abcnews.go.com/US/seung-hui-chos-mental-health-records-released/story?id=8278195

p. 83: "That's probably the scariest . . ." Evan Thomas, "Making of a Massacre," *Newsweek* (April 29, 2007). http://www.thedailybeast.com/newsweek/2007/04/29/making-of-a-massacre.html

GLOSSaRY

affidavit—a sworn statement, in writing, that sets out a person's testimony.

feckless—irresponsible or incompetent.

felony—a serious crime; in the United States, a felony is any crime for which the punishment is more than one year in prison or the death penalty.

paranoia—a mental disorder characterized by the strong belief that the person is being unfairly persecuted.

parole—releasing someone sentenced to prison before the full sentence is served, granted for good behavior.

poseur—a person who pretends to be something he or she is not.

pro bono—a Latin phrase meaning "for the public good," referring to legal work undertaken without payment or at a reduced fee as a public service.

psychological profile—a list of personality traits that describes the likely perpetrator of a crime, based on the analysis of evidence from similar crimes.

psychopath—an individual exhibiting a set of antisocial personality traits and behaviors, including compulsive lying, failure to accept responsibility for personal actions, extreme narcissism, lack of empathy, impulsivity, and lack of guilt or remorse.

psychosis—a loss of contact with reality, as evidenced by hallucinations, delusions, or disordered speech or behavior.

schizophrenia—a serious, chronic brain disorder characterized by delusional thinking and behavior, often accompanied by auditory or visual hallucinations.

SWAT—acronym for "Special Weapons and Tactics," a term used for police units that use military-style weapons and tactics. SWAT units are typically called in for high-risk engagements that are beyond the capability of regular police units to handle properly.

Valium—a medication used to treat anxiety and other medical conditions.

FURTHER READING

Bernstein, Arnie. *Bath Massacre: America's First School Bombing*. Ann Arbor: University of Michigan Press, 2009.

Cullen, Dave. *Columbine*. New York: Twelve, 2009.

Duwe, Grant. *Mass Murder in the United States: A History*. Jefferson, NC: McFarland, 2007.

Fox, James Alan, and Jack Levin. *Extreme Killing: Understanding Serial and Mass Murder*. Thousand Oaks, CA: SAGE Publications, 2005.

Lavergne, Gary M. *A Sniper in the Tower: The Charles Whitman Murders*. Denton: University of North Texas Press, 1997.

Newman, Katherine S. *Rampage: The Social Roots of School Shootings*. New York: Basic Books, 2005.

Ressler, Robert K., and Tom Schachtman. *Whoever Fights Monsters*. New York: St. Martin's Paperbacks, 1992.

Roy, Lucinda. *No Right to Remain Silent: The Tragedy at Virginia Tech*. New York: Crown Books, 2009.

INTERNET RESOURCES

http://www.columbine-online.com/

The companion website to journalist Dave Cullen's acclaimed book *Columbine* features samples of the killers' writing; video, still photos, and diagrams of the crime scene; a police synopsis of the "Basement Tapes"; and more.

http://www.motherjones.com/politics/2012/07/mass-shootings-map

Mother Jones magazine's brief guide to mass shootings in America contains summary information, an interactive map, graphs, a timeline, and links to articles and data tables.

http://www.fbi.gov/stats-services/publications/school-shooter

An FBI report on school shooters.

http://timelines.latimes.com/deadliest-shooting-rampages/

This interactive timeline from the *Los Angeles Times* covers the deadliest mass shootings in the United States, from 1998 to the present. A summary, photo of the offender, and link to an original story in the *Times* is included for each incident.

http://www.oprah.com/world/Susan-Klebolds-O-Magazine-Essay-I-Will-Never-Know-Why

An essay written for O *Magazine* by Susan Klebold, the mother of one of the Columbine shooters.

http://www.biography.com/people/andrew-kehoe-235986

The television program A&E Biography provides information about Andrew Kehoe and the 1927 Bath School bombing.

http://www.trutv.com/library/crime/notorious_murders/mass/index.html

The Crime Library website includes articles about notorious mass murderers and spree killers, including Eric Harris and Dylan Klebold, Jared Lee Loughner, Richard Speck, and Charles Whitman.

http://www.texasmonthly.com/2006-08-01/feature.php

Text and photos from the article "96 Minutes," published in *Texas Monthly* in August 2006, the 40th anniversary of Charles Whitman's Texas Tower shooting rampage.

http://carolynmccarthy.house.gov/gun-safety3/

This page on U.S. Rep. Carolyn McCarthy's website details the New York congresswoman's policies on gun safety. McCarthy was elected to Congress after the murder of her husband, Dennis, by Long Island Rail Road shooter Colin Ferguson in December 1993.

http://www.nbcnews.com/id/18138369/

NBC News coverage of the Virginia Tech massacre in 2007 includes links to stories, as well as photos and videos sent to the news agency by the killer, Seung-Hui Cho.

INDEX

Numbers in **bold italics** refer to captions

About the Author: Rudolph T. Heits is the author of several books for young adults, including *Communism* (Mason Crest, 2012). He is from Texas.